INSIGHT INTO

SELF-HARM

Helena Wilkinson and Abbie Robson

CWR

Published 2014 by CWR, Waverley Abbey House, Waverley Lane, Farnham, Surrey GU9 8EP UK. Registered Charity No. 294387. Registered Limited Company No. 1990308.

For list of National Distributors visit our website www.cwr.org.uk

Unless otherwise indicated, all Scripture references are from the Holy Bible: New International Version (NIV), copyright © 1973, 1978, 1984 by the International Bible Society.

Other translations used:

TLB: *The Living Bible*, © 1971, 1994, Tyndale House Publishers

GNB: Good News Bible © 1994 published by the Bible Societies/HarperCollins Publishers Ltd UK, Good News Bible© American Bible Society 1966, 1971, 1976, 1992. Used with permission

NASB: New American Standard Bible. Copyright © 1960, 1962, 1963, 1968, 1971, 1972, 1973, 1975, 1977, 1995 by the Lockman Foundation. Used by permission.

Concept development, editing, design and production by CWR

Printed in the UK by Page Bros.

ISBN: 978-1-85345-960-3

WAVERLEY ABBEY
INSIGHT SERIES

The *Waverley Abbey Insight Series* has been developed in response to the great need to help people understand and face some key issues that many of us struggle with today. CWR's ministry spans teaching, training and publishing, and this series draws on all of these areas of ministry.

Sourced from material first presented over Insight Days by CWR at their base, Waverley Abbey House, presenters and authors have worked in close co-operation to bring this series together, offering clear insight, teaching and help on a broad range of subjects and issues. Bringing biblical understanding and godly insight, these books are written both for those who help others and those who face these issues themselves.

Dedication

This book is dedicated to all those who have battled, or continue to do so, with self-harm. Don't give up the fight to recover.

Thanks

Our grateful thanks go to Chris Ledger for her insights, Nikki Cole for all her hard work in shaping this book and John Robson for casting a careful eye over it.

Disclaimer

Insights come from personal and professional experience, research and interviews with self-harmers. The information given is accurate to the best of our knowledge.

Other books by Helena Wilkinson

Puppet on a String (Horsham: RoperPenberthy Publishing, 2004); *Snakes & Ladders* (Horsham: RoperPenberthy Publishing, 2007); *Beyond Chaotic Eating* (Horsham: RoperPenberthy Publishing, 2001); *Beyond Singleness* (Horsham: RoperPenberthy Publishing, 2007); *A Way out of Despair* (Farnham: CWR, 1995); *Breaking Free from Loneliness* (Horsham: RoperPenberthy Publishing, 2004); *Insight into Eating Disorders* (Farnham: CWR, 2006); *Inspiring Women – Finding Freedom*, (Farnham: CWR, 2007); *Designed for Living*, Jeannette Barwick and Helena Wilkinson (Farnham: CWR, 2009). Available through Amazon. Titles published by CWR can also be ordered from www.cwr.org.uk/store

CONTENTS

INTRODUCTION

According to a report in the *Guardian* (27 July 2004) from an NHS watchdog, the number of Britons deliberately harming themselves is reaching 'epidemic' levels. Over 170,000 people visit accident and emergency departments each year for help with 'self-injury'.[1] Even higher numbers will never appear as part of the statistics because they self-harm in secret. Unless the stigma is broken and self-harm is sufficiently addressed, the numbers will inevitably go on increasing.

There have been many myths around self-harm and the self-harmer is often misunderstood. I (Abbie) was a self-harmer for many years and remember well the terrifying world into which I became locked. One day, instead of resorting to my usual strategy of perfect, fine cuts on various parts of my body, I was consumed by the desire to splinter my shin with a hammer. I was so shocked and terrified that I might carry it out that I rang the charity that Helena was running and spoke to someone to say I didn't know how long I could keep up the charade of everything being OK. It was the start of my road to recovery. I recalled my struggles in my book, *Secret Scars*, and went on to train in counselling and set up Adullam Ministries – an online support and information resource.

I (Helena) first came across self-harm at the age of twenty shortly after my first book, *Puppet on a String*, an account of my battle to overcome anorexia, was published. I used to meet with young people with eating disorders to encourage them. One day I went to the home of a girl who confessed that she had cut herself so badly that her pyjamas had stuck to her arm. I was horrified that a youngster could be in the same house as her parents and inflict such injuries upon herself. Years later, when I trained in counselling and set up a charity for eating disorder sufferers, I realised how many people self-harm. I also acknowledged that the hair pulling, scratching of my wrists and occasional cut I carried out as a teenager meant that I too had self-harmed in some small way. So together we offer you our insights from personal and professional experience.

Insight into Self-Harm aims to bring awareness and answers to those suffering and caring. It is divided into three parts:

Part 1 explores the nature of self-harm, who suffers and the underlying causes.

Part 2 addresses the path to recovery, including the physical, emotional and spiritual aspects.

Part 3 offers tips for dealing with relapse and for those helping in different settings.

We suggest that you read all the chapters as together they make up the whole; but if at any time you feel a bit overwhelmed by what you read, put the book down and do something a little more light-hearted, returning when you are ready.

If you are a self-harmer, we recommend that you purchase a large notebook with dividers, as throughout the chapters we make suggestions of written exercises to aid your recovery. You might want to name your notebook and personalise the cover, perhaps adding photos, drawings, doodles and words.

Whatever your reason for reading the book, it is our desire that what we have written will offer hope. If you are still stuck in the lonely, dark, miry pit of self-harm, hold onto the fact that others have travelled this path, too, and have recovered. If you are a family member or friend then we urge you to stick by the person however tough it is to do so. If you are helping someone in a professional capacity, then we encourage you to explore all avenues; address the reasons behind the self-harm and offer keys to coping with life's hurdles. We need to understand self-harm and self-harmers. It is our hope that this book will not only open your eyes to what goes on behind self-harm, but will offer tools and hope for recovery.

Helena Wilkinson & Abbie Robson, 2013

NOTES
[1]www.selfinjurysupport.org.uk/about-self-injury

CHAPTER 1

WHAT IS SELF-HARM?

THE CRY TO BE UNDERSTOOD

Self-harm is not a comfortable subject. As a self-harmer you can feel shocked, guilty or frightened of what others may think when you realise that injuring yourself has become more than a one-off incident. As a person who does not self-harm, when you first discover someone is hurting themselves, sometimes in horrifying ways, your response can be one of dismay and panic: you feel powerless about what to do for the best or hindered by not being able to sufficiently identify with such actions. Lack of insight, understanding and compassion lead many sufferers to hide what is happening and consequently not receive adequate help.

Debbie says

'Very early on as a self-harmer, I told my youth leader what I was doing. She saw it as attention seeking behaviour and something I could easily stop if I wanted. I didn't speak about it again until one day I found myself in A&E having cut so badly I needed stitches. I often wonder if it would have got to this stage if my youth leader had understood and I'd had some help.'

Debbie's cry was, 'If only someone understood my world.' Many continue to fight the battle alone, desperate to feel understood and to be helped through the overwhelming feelings and devastating consequences of self-harm. Perhaps you are one of those people or maybe you are a concerned parent, partner or friend of someone who self-harms.

'It is estimated that between one in twelve and one in fifteen young people in the UK now self-harm and the UK is said to have the highest rate of self-harm in Europe.'[1] In 2012, ChildLine reported that self-harm is the leading concern amongst fourteen-year-olds who contact them, and that there has been a 68 per cent increase in the number of children phoning or emailing about self-harm. Sadly, according to a 2008 report in the *Observer*, children as young as five are self-harming and many people continue harming beyond their teens and twenties. Some people even begin to self-harm later in life. Both men and women are affected by self-harm, although the majority of self-harmers are young women.

Dan says

'I have self-harmed since I was five years old. I cut the soles of my feet with knives and blades and sometimes I can't walk and have to make excuses. I was born to much older parents who were disabled and always shouting at each other. I felt I had nowhere to escape. I started comfort eating and then used to play with my feet huddled up on the sofa. One day I developed a blister and I picked it. I liked the pain and blood – it felt like a release – so I started cutting my feet with a penknife and still do today, now aged forty-eight. I've been warned by several doctors about septicaemia, but the need is hard wired in my brain and self-harm is a compelling escape.'

IDENTIFYING WITH SELF-HARM

Self-harm is a drastic measure and it can be hard to understand how someone could injure their body to the extreme that many do. Unless we can identify in some way with those who self-harm, we are in danger of giving out negative vibes, whether we mean to or not. However, we have all, no doubt, been through experiences that are not dissimilar to self-harm in the effect they create. Whilst I (Abbie) was running a workshop on self-harm for counsellors, I threw in a couple of questions they weren't expecting: 'How many of you have self-harmed?' I asked. As I expected, no one answered.

'How many of you have slammed a door because you were frustrated during an argument, or bitten your lip to stop yourself from crying, or thumped a table when you felt no one was listening?' A few hands went up, and more wavered as they began to see my point; we use our bodies in response to our feelings even if we don't go to the extreme of becoming a self-harmer through actions like picking the skin around our fingers in response to anxiety or to punish ourselves, or by hitting an object or kicking a wall. Nor do we deprive ourselves because we feel annoyed or undeserving, or drink too much to dull pain.

When we realise that we, too, have encountered the connection between negative emotions and physical reactions as a means of relief or punishment, it brings self-harm into the realm of an understandable experience. Our lack of shock or revulsion at self-harm helps sufferers to be more willing to share their experiences rather than hide a 'forbidden act' for fear of repercussions or being labelled 'mentally unstable'.

PAUSE FOR THOUGHT

Do you need to change the way you see self-harm? Are you a counsellor, pastor, parent, partner or friend, maybe with preconceived ideas? Or are you a sufferer who has lived with guilt, secrecy and self-hatred and who now needs to be a bit kinder to yourself?

DEFINING SELF-HARM

What comes to mind when people talk about self-harm? There are many types of self-harm that we will explore shortly and several different terminologies used to describe people who harm themselves: self-injury, self-injurious behaviour, self-harm, deliberate self-harm, self-mutilation and para-suicide, amongst others. Whilst there may be slight differences, they all express injury in response to emotional needs.

There are some forms of self-harm ('psychotic' and 'organic') related to schizophrenia, autistic disorders, developmental disabilities, and some psychologically induced disorders, but this book will concentrate on what is known as 'typical' self-harm – harming as a physical response to emotional pain.

Whilst self-harm has been spoken and written about for centuries (appearing in Sophocles' play, *Oedipus the King* around 430 BC as well as in the Bible), it was not recognised as a condition in its own right until recently. In medical books it tends to be listed as occurring in conjunction with conditions such as eating disorders and borderline personality disorder. This has left people without such a diagnosis feeling as if their experience isn't valid. Perhaps you have felt like this at times?

The new edition of *Diagnostic and Statistical Manual of Mental Disorders* (DSM-5),[2] lists a condition called NSSI Disorder ('Non-Suicidal Self Injury Disorder'). This has at least helped to give a voice to people who struggle solely with self-harm. NSSI disorder explains self-harm as an emotional coping mechanism rather than faulty brain wiring or evidence of psychosis. It describes a person who engages in intentional self-inflicted damage to the surface of their body to induce bleeding, bruising or pain, without intending to commit suicide and as a result of negative feelings and thoughts.

THE SECRECY OF SELF-HARM

Self-harm is a secret world for most sufferers, with desperate attempts to hide what is happening. By its very nature it is isolating and can be extremely hard to admit. The fear in being open and honest is that people will make judgments and act differently, which, sadly, is largely true.

Not only is the self-harm itself carefully concealed, but the reasons for it too, with the sufferer hiding things from both others and themselves (especially when trauma has been pushed into the subconscious). Many people feel shame about their self-harm: shame not only about what they do but what has led them to do it.

> Helen says
> 'I didn't believe that my feelings were valid so I couldn't speak about what was going on, yet I hurt so deeply. Self-harm became a visible expression of what was happening inside. It was a secret place; a protective cocoon that I could escape to that no one else need know about. I think it was addictive because it was secretive. It fed my desire to carry on looking as if I could cope with life, and not bother other people.'

SIGNS OF SELF-HARM

How do you know if someone is a self-harmer? There are signs you can look out for and changes in a person's conduct that are 'giveaways', such as:

- Injuries that seem to defy the explanation given ('I fell over', 'my cat scratched me', etc).
- Uncharacteristic defensiveness: growing more and more guarded, anxious and vague when asked about scratches, cuts, burns or scars.
- Insistence on wearing long sleeves, long skirts and trousers regardless of the weather – many self-harmers say that people first found out about their self-harm during the summer months.

- Behavioural changes: appearing distracted, preoccupied, distant or emotionally absent. In addition, sufferers may have need to spend more time retreating to their own private space (to injure themselves).
- Sharp objects and implements lying around or amongst the person's belongings that didn't used to be there (razors, knives, scissors, bits of glass, bottle caps, etc).

When you know what you are looking for the signs are fairly obvious, but some people go to great lengths to hide the fact that they are self-harming.

> Alex says
> 'If you saw me walking down the road you would never know I self-harm. I'm a professional who wears suits to work and has a busy social life. Cutting is something I do on my own in the places no one sees. If people knew I'd probably lose my job.'

> Lucy says
> 'I never got any of my cuts stitched, even though I know I should have done, because I was afraid of being thrown out of medical school if anyone found out.'

The easiest way to find out if someone you care about is self-harming is to ask them! You may find that they either deny it or don't want to talk to you about it, but at least you will have been able to let them know that you care enough to ask.

WAYS PEOPLE SELF-HARM

Self-harm describes a whole host of behaviours that people carry out to hurt themselves. Matthew Nock points out that: 'It is important to distinguish between directly self-injurious behaviors (eg, self-injury, suicide) and indirectly harmful behaviors (eg, alcohol and substance use); however, these different forms of self-harm commonly co-occur, and it may be useful to consider them on a continuum of self-harm behaviors.'[3] We (the authors) have chosen to classify directly self-harming behaviour as external and internal.

External self-harm

Cutting: This is also known as slicing or slashing and is done with a knife, razor blade, broken glass/china, or other sharp objects. It is most commonly carried out on the wrists, arms and legs, but can also include the stomach, face, neck, feet, breasts and genitals.

Burning/scalding: This is usually done with cigarettes, lighters, matches, kitchen hobs, heated objects, irons, radiators, boiling water or steam. Sometimes people use chemicals to burn themselves or assist the burning (gasoline, propane, alcohol, and lighter fluid, etc).

Cold burns: These are a part of burning and can be even more damaging. They include the use of aerosols (eg deodorants) or compressed gases (eg balloon helium canisters). More rarely, they will involve the use of dry ice or liquid nitrogen.

Hitting: This usually involves the person head banging or inflicting blows to their head, thighs or other parts of their body with their fists.

Hair-pulling (Trichotillomania): This is excessive and

recurrent removal of a person's own hair resulting in a noticeable loss. Usually the hair is removed from the scalp, eyebrows or beard.

Biting: This is usually done to the arms, hands or fingers, including excessive and severe nail biting. People can bite their fingernails so much that they draw blood and damage the nails.

Scratching: This is more extreme in frequency, intensity and duration than ordinary scratching. It can lead to the skin becoming raw, which can result in bleeding. It is usually done with the fingernails but sometimes with a sharp or semi-sharp object.

Breaking bones: This is a drastic and less common form of self-injury. Usually people break their bones with an instrument such as a hammer or other heavy object but they may also purposely throw themselves down stairs or into walls or doors.

Interfering with wounds: Some pick and scratch at wounds; others remove stitches prematurely, stick objects such as needles or pins into the wounds or reopen them by other means.

Internal self-harm

Swallowing/inserting objects: This may involve swallowing foreign objects or inserting them in the orifices of the body, such as the genitals. Inserting sharp objects under the skin or even draining blood with a syringe can also be used.

Ingesting harmful substances: This can include ingesting poisonous substances, such as bleach, or taking an overdose of prescription/non-prescription medication intended to cause harm but not to kill.

There are other ways in which people harm themselves.

When you think of the words 'self-harm' would you include the following?

- over/under eating
- alcohol/drug abuse
- excessive smoking
- dangerous driving
- not looking after emotional/physical needs
- extreme risk taking
- staying in abusive relationships
- choosing unsafe sex with a view of risk

Types of self-harmers

In addition to the various methods people use, there are also different types of self-harmers:

Compulsive: You feel compelled to self-harm and a voice inside says, 'do it ... do it ... you have to do it'. You feel driven, and if you ignore the craving, it just gets worse; you feel as if you have no choice. You become preoccupied with the thought and fearful that if you don't self-harm something bad will happen.

Impulsive: You get a sudden urge to self-harm – you must do it *right now*. You probably don't self-harm on a regular basis and when you do it may be under the influence of alcohol.

Ritualistic: You might feel that you can relate to the description of compulsive self-harm but you also have a ritual that is associated with it. You take time to plan your self-harm act; organising both the implements and the First Aid equipment needed to deal with the injuries. This may involve laying them out neatly and creating the right atmosphere (playing music, lighting a candle, etc), resulting in feeling relaxed, soothed and sleepy.

If you self-harm, in which category do you think you fit? No matter what the nature of self-harm, it is increasing and very much a part of current life with its broken relationships, choices and pressures.

REFLECTION

The only way we are going to break the stigma surrounding self-harm is by talking about it. The more we discuss it, the less hidden it becomes.

ACTION

We've talked about various types of self-harm. Which of these had you not considered as self-harm but now realise are a part of what you have done or still do? Write them down and, if possible, tell someone who understands.

If you don't self-harm, can you think of ways in which you use physical sensation to deal with emotion?

PRAYER

Dear God, please help me to break the secrecy around my self-harm (or to be aware of the self-harming of those close to me). Thank You Jesus that You are the light of the world, shining into the dark places and that nothing is secret with You. Amen.

CHAPTER 2

SELF-HARM: WHO AND WHY?

A CROSS-SECTION OF PEOPLE

What type of person comes to mind when you think of self-harm? An emotionally unstable woman in need of psychiatric help? A young person who doesn't know how to cope? A teenager copying her friends who self-harm? A prisoner lashing out in anger at himself? A goth, making a statement? In fact anyone could potentially become a self-harmer, although those who have gone through traumatic experiences and/or those who suffer from certain mental illnesses are more likely to self-harm. Until their stories became public, I wonder if you would have considered Kelly Holmes, Victoria Pendleton, Angelina Jolie, Richey Edwards and Princess Diana as self-harmers?[1]

Kelly Holmes, OBE, athlete and Olympic gold medalist, fell into a deep depression after suffering a number of leg injuries. 'With each cut I felt I was punishing myself but at the same time I felt a sense of release that drove me to do it again and again.'

Victoria Pendleton, cyclist and Olympic gold medalist, has revealed how she turned to self-harm while battling the pressures of competing, even cutting herself on the night she won her first gold medal in Beijing.

Angelina Jolie, Academy Award winning actress, used to hurt herself during her early teens but stopped around the age of sixteen. 'I was trying to feel something. I really hurt myself. I nearly cut my jugular vein.'

Richey Edwards, lyricist and rhythm guitarist of the rock band Manic Street Preachers, suffered from severe depression and self-harm. He said, 'When I cut myself I feel so much better … I'm not a person who can scream and shout so this is my only outlet.'

Diana, Princess of Wales, revealed to the world in a BBC television interview (1995) that she was a self-harmer. She said that she had cut her arms and legs, explaining, 'You have so much pain inside yourself that you try and hurt yourself on the outside because you want help.'

WHO SELF-HARMS?

The Royal College of Psychiatry states that self-harm happens more often in:

- young women
- prisoners, asylum seekers, and veterans of the armed forces
- gay, lesbian and bisexual people: this seems, at least in part, due to the stress of prejudice and discrimination
- a group of young people who self-harm together: having a friend who self-harms may increase your chances of doing it as well
- people who have experienced physical, emotional or sexual abuse during childhood.

Common problems include physical or sexual abuse or relationship problems with partners, friends, and family. Self-harming can also be triggered by being unemployed, having difficulties at work, or feeling depressed or bad about yourself. You may also be more likely to harm yourself if you feel that people don't listen to you, if you feel hopeless, isolated, alone or out of control, or if you feel powerless, as though there's nothing you can do to change anything.[2]

THE ROLE OF SELF-HARM

If asked to describe their self-harm, sufferers are much more likely to talk about the role it plays, perhaps because this is more significant than the injuries themselves, such as:

'It's my inner scream.'

'It helps me feel alive.'

'It's the way I cope.'

'It's a way to express my emotions.'

'It's my voice when I don't have words.'

'It's the only way to exert control over my body.'

'It stops me thinking.'

'It's a way to feel empowered.'

'It gives me a rush of endorphins.'

'It's a response to peer pressure.'

'It's cleansing – getting rid of bad blood.'

PAUSE FOR THOUGHT

If you self-harm, which of the above statements ring true? If you are helping someone, which would be more appropriate? Perhaps understanding the role self-harm plays will enable you to pinpoint key areas that need addressing. The following cross section of stories reveals some of the causes and roles of self-harm. Perhaps you can identify with one or two of them.

Sophie, aged 21, says
'I was bullied and left out at school; each time the insults and exclusion happened I got more fragile and sensitive. Self-harm calmed me down and gave me a "sudden rush". After that I needed it more and more.'

Claire, aged 15, says
'When I first started cutting it was because I'd read about it and was curious. I felt guilty. Now I do it to punish myself, especially if I think I've hurt someone else.'

Tom, aged 29, says
'In the army I witnessed people being killed and nearly lost my own life. I began to suffer from depression, anxiety and flashbacks and was diagnosed with Post Traumatic Stress Disorder (PTSD). Self-harm helps me come back to the present.'

Alison, aged 24, says
'I've had bulimia for six years and I also self-harm. Whenever the bulimia starts to get better, the self-harm gets worse. I think it's the same thing – my way of coping – but it just comes out in a different way.'

Marco, aged 25, says

'I do drugs and when I can't do drugs, I cut. I like it and I don't want to stop. I sometimes get drunk specifically to cut; it's an incredible feeling.'

Pam, aged 38, says

'I have recently started therapy for childhood abuse. I dissociate and sometimes self-harm during this time, but I often don't remember self-harming and feel shocked when I see the cuts.'

WHY SELF-HARM?

Research has shown that most people self-harm in order to help regulate internal experiences such as emotions, thoughts, memories and physical sensations. Sufferers have said that besides escaping emotional pain, self-harm slows down racing thoughts, ends a dissociative episode and gives a sense of control. In fact, for most self-harmers the act of hurting themselves serves many different functions depending on what is going on in their life at the time.

People don't self-harm because they *want to* but because they *need to*. When you understand why, it doesn't necessarily stop the self-harm but allows the person to gain insight into the causes, understand the purpose it serves and realise that there are other, healthy ways of obtaining the pain-relieving/calming effect.

The reasons that people self-harm can be broadly grouped into four categories, each of which is considered in detail.

1. RESPONSE TO EMOTIONS

We all respond to emotions in different ways; at times we respond well and at other times not so well. This is due, in part, to our upbringing, life skills, personality, history and trauma experiences. If we are emotionally healthy, we may have days when something gets to us and we walk out in a mood, slam a door or flick on the TV to switch off from uncomfortable feelings, but it's relatively mild and infrequent compared to someone in a lot of emotional pain.

Most self-harmers have difficulty with emotional regulation: the ability to respond to demands in life with a range of emotions and to delay spontaneous reactions when needed. They find it extremely difficult to know what to do with negative emotions and are easily overwhelmed. Alternatively they feel numb and need to feel 'something' so injure themselves in order to feel real.

The chart on the next page shows two common pathways to self-harm (injury) in response to emotional overload and emotional numbness.[3]

TWO COMMON PATHWAYS TO SELF-INJURY

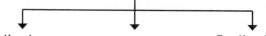

Emotional overload

Emotions become:
Too real
Out of control
Overwhelming

Person feels:
Unable to cope
About to explode/ disintegrate

↓

Person self-injures
Goal: To shift the focus from internal to external, thus re-establishing a sense of emotional balance

↓

Consequences
Sense of calm and relief from overwhelming emotions

Person feels:
Better
More in control
More able to cope and function

Vacillation

Individual may waver/swing from emotional overload to emotional numbness

This process can happen almost instinctively and the person may or may not be aware of the process.

'Self-injury is a sure-fire way of controlling my emotions so they don't overwhelm me. It's something I do to myself, for myself, and it gives me a sense of control.'

'I feel relief when the blood flows: it shows me I'm alive and it shows me the emotional pain I feel is real.'

'It usually feels like someone else has taken over or like a dazed out feel.'

Emotional numbness

(Dissociative state)
Individual enters a depersonalised, derealised or trance-like state.

Person feels:
Detached
Dead inside
Unreal

↓

Person self-injures
Goal: To terminate the distressing dissociative episode

↓

Consequences
Sense of aliveness and confirmation of existence

Person thinks/ feels:
I do exist
I am real/alive
More grounded in the present and more able to cope and function

The term dissociation refers to a state in which an integrated part of a person's life becomes separated from the rest of the personality and functions independently through thoughts, feelings and memories.

People who self-harm tend to reach a point of overload more easily and resort to dramatic responses. For example, a person with social anxiety may clench their hands to avoid shaking as they endeavour to talk with someone in a social setting. An alcoholic may drink themselves into oblivion following a highly stressful situation. Anorexics who feel controlled by others may cut back on eating because they feel it is the only area of their lives they can control. People with obsessive-compulsive disorder may experience intense anxiety regarding cleanliness and wash their hands until they bleed.

The emotions with which the self-harmer tends to become overloaded are anger, anxiety and sadness. Guilt and shame also play key parts in keeping the self-harm cycle going round, as we will explore in Chapter 4.

Anger
Anger is a natural emotion that helps us to deal with challenges and threats in life; it protects us from potential harm. However, it can also be very destructive. One of the key factors behind anger is *loss of control / blocked goal.*

Anger in itself isn't bad; it's how we respond that can be damaging. Burying it leads to feelings of worthlessness and depression; lashing out at others leads to hurt. The best approach to dealing with anger is to seek to understand why it is there, to respect it and to express it without hurting yourself or others.

If you need further help to understand and to learn how to

deal with anger in a constructive way, the organisation Mind will be able to help.[4] Visit www.mind.org.uk or call the infoline on 0300 123 3393 and ask for a leaflet.

Anxiety

The Calm Clinic for panic and anxiety sufferers makes an interesting point about the connection between anger and anxiety. They call it the 'hidden anxiety emotion' and say that few people realise that anger can be an outcome of anxiety or fear. Anxiety has various physical symptoms (feeling dizzy, shaking, rapid heartbeat, etc) and it can also cause a person to imagine that things in their life are worse than they really are. Some of the most common psychological symptoms (the thoughts or altered perceptions we have) of anxiety are thinking or feeling that:

- we may lose control and/or go 'mad'
- we might die
- we may have a heart attack/be sick/faint/have a brain tumour
- people are looking at us and observing our anxiety
- things are speeding up/slowing down
- we are detached from our environment and the people in it
- we want to run away/escape from the situation
- we are on edge and alert to everything around us

For more information about anxiety, visit www.helpguide.org

Sadness

Sadness is emotional pain associated with feeling low and experiencing moments of despair, sorrow or helplessness. It comes and goes; most people experience it at times. An intense feeling of prolonged sadness is classed as depression. Clinical depression is a more serious form of depression in which the mood lasts for most of the day, is more pronounced in the morning and which is marked by loss of interest in everyday life and relationships.

It is important that medical help is sought for depression. It is also necessary to learn the skills needed to manage stress and balance emotions. www.helpguide.org offers an online self-guided programme to help you to deal with stress and to enable you to take control of your life.

2. TYPE OF COMMUNICATION

When I (Helena) am working with eating disorder sufferers or equipping others to do so, I ask a key question: 'If your eating disorder had a voice, what would it say?' The same question can be asked of self-harm. Write down your reply. If you are helping someone then try the exercise with them. The answers people have given include:

'I need help, but I don't know how to ask or express that need.'

'I need help but I don't even know what I need help for.'

'I hate myself so much I must hurt myself.'

'I need scars because they are a sign of the different people who have hurt me.'

'I don't deserve help, but I wish someone would ask what's wrong.'

'It makes my pain legitimate.'

'I am weak, hopeless, a failure.'

'It just proves that I'm the disgusting person I said I was.'

'I need power and control I don't have in other ways.'

'I can't cope … I'm in distress.'

'I don't feel safe … I need to feel safe.'

'I have needs, I'm hurting, I want to be cared for.'

'I need space in my head because it's full and it hurts.'

Looking back on her self-harm, Hannah says something very significant. Perhaps you or someone you know can identify with this: 'I felt like I needed stitches; to be sewn up like an old toy. It proved to me I needed fixing and I was fragile.'

3. MEANS OF RE-ENACTMENT

People who self-harm have often been through traumatic experiences and therefore it can be a form of trauma re-enactment (bringing about the feelings they felt when first traumatised). 'Why on earth would someone want to do that?' you may ask. It's like an inbuilt reaction. When in shock, animals that have been traumatised tend to return to the container in which the incident occurred in preference to less familiar locations. In the same way, some people who have been traumatised seem to 'need' pain. They follow similar patterns to the trauma encountered; familiarity appears to provide comfort.

Debbie used to re-create situations where she was alone and physically hurt or in danger, such as cutting or overdosing, in order to be found by someone who would call for help. She would re-live the physical and emotional trauma of past abuse but experience the 'looked after' ending to the scenario that she had never had as a child. The need to carry out this pattern in the end became highly addictive.

4. PHYSIOLOGICAL REACTION

Part of the reason why a person self-harms may be related to brain functioning. Research shows that self-harmers have low levels of serotonin (involved in regulating emotion, mood, impulsivity, aggression, digestion, smooth muscle relaxation, and sexual behaviour, among other functions). Scientists think that problems in the serotonin system may predispose some people to self-injury.

Endorphins, neurotransmitters in the brain, are created and released when someone self-harms (they are also released in other circumstances such as exercise). These neurotransmitters trigger opiate receptors located in the brain, causing those receptors to produce heightened feelings of pleasure, well-being and numbness to pain, temporarily releasing emotional turmoil. It is said that this natural high is not unlike the highs produced by narcotics, such as cocaine, opium and methamphetamine, which also trigger addictions. After a few self-harming episodes, studies suggest it is possible for a person to become addicted to the resulting and powerful euphoria.

REFLECTION

Anyone can fall prey to self harm, from any age group or walk of life – even those we most revere. Let's remember that no one wants to self-harm – it's a need that must be met, in whatever way is possible.

ACTION

If you have already answered the question 'If my self-harm had a voice what would it say' see if you can expand on what you wrote. Something physical, like a piece of paper, helps to make a problem more tangible and less hidden.

PRAYER

Dear God, please help me to understand the purpose of my self-harming (or that of those I care about). Please help me to believe that there are other ways of coping; it won't be like this forever. Amen.

CHAPTER 3

THE DEEPER ISSUES

MORE THAN MEETS THE EYE

People tend to shy away from helping those who self-harm because of the complexities of the issue. Many do not understand that self-harm is not actually the problem: it is the person's solution to many problems in their life. This is why sufferers can feel threatened if self-harming is prevented in some way. We need to grasp that self-harm, like any addiction, has root causes. These deeper issues can be due to trauma, lack of life skills or a part of a physiological or psychological illness.

In most cases self-harm is a combination of many factors, both external and internal: experiences outside the person that trigger self-harm and the internal battles that maintain it. For example, someone might endure the trauma of being bullied in addition to a lack of confidence, fear about the adult world and negative beliefs about herself.

Below are listed the different aspects that contribute towards someone becoming a self-harmer and hence need addressing if they are to stop.

Predisposing situations: unmet childhood needs; trauma and life experiences.

Co-existing problems: disorders and addictions; lack of life skills.

External pressures: echoes of the past; changes in circumstances.

Internal battles: feelings and fears; thoughts and beliefs.

Let's look at each one in more detail.

PREDISPOSING SITUATIONS

Unmet childhood needs

Many people who self-harm have not experienced the solid building blocks necessary to grow into a confident and independent adult. There are a number of essentials, of which children need a *sufficient* amount, to best prepare them to handle life well in adulthood, even though their lives will be interjected by some negative experiences (no parent is perfect). The easiest way to remember the key building blocks is by the acronym PARENTS.[1]

Protection: It's crucial that all children feel safe and secure. They need a sense of order and predictability, routine, peace and stability within which they can learn to trust others and build relationships.

Acceptance: All children need to be accepted, loved and cherished for who they are. Parents should reflect back to their children the world's perception of them, telling them that they are valuable and worthy, so that their children learn to value and believe in themselves.

Recognition: Many children like to please their parents; they love to be realistically praised and to hear their parents say: 'I'm so proud of you. You did a fabulous job.' This helps them evaluate their worth and so can enhance their ability to progress in life.

Enforced Limits: Children need a sense of predictability. They need to see that rules are followed so that life is *not* chaotic. If boundaries are fluid, the world can feel scary and may not make much sense.

Nearness: Expressing love is crucial for communicating love, so children need to be held and hugged by their parents. This sends the powerful message that their needs matter, and their parents care for them.

Time: Children need to spend time in their parents' presence and to have their full attention, as this sends the message 'I like being with you.' They then are more likely to believe that others will like and want them, too.

Support: For children, the outside world can sometimes be a scary place with unknown dangers and unmet challenges. Hence they may need their parents' encouragement, affirmation and support to venture into and explore the outside world in order to develop independence and increasing autonomy.

Trauma and life experiences

We tend to think that for someone who self-harms there must have been a major trauma, especially given the terrible injuries that some people inflict. Whilst some have endured deep trauma, others experience a build up of smaller traumas that can nevertheless have an equally devastating effect, putting the person in a position of feeling unable to cope. Others have experienced very little trauma but due to their sensitive nature find it hard to deal with what may be perceived by some as quite ordinary challenges.

Emotional and psychological trauma is the result of extraordinarily stressful events that shatter your sense of security, making you feel helpless and vulnerable in a dangerous world. Common traumas include:

- physical abuse and witnessing violence
- physical/psychological neglect
- sexual abuse and rape
- teasing about puberty or fear/shame about sexuality
- emotional and verbal abuse
- enforced role reversal (child being the parent)
- bullying, physical or emotional
- extreme lack of communication
- loss/separation
- parental illness/alcoholism
- broken family relationships
- break up of significant friendships/relationships
- poor handling of disabilities

An event is most likely to lead to emotional or psychological trauma if it happens unexpectedly, if you are unprepared for it or if you feel powerless to prevent it. Trauma is also more likely to be the outcome of an event if it happens repeatedly, is the result of intentional cruelty or if it occurs in childhood. The effects of childhood trauma and many of the co-existing problems we are about to explore are associated with such trauma.

CO-EXISTING PROBLEMS

Disorders and addictions

Alongside self-harm the person may suffer from one or more of the following (this is not an exclusive list):

Depression: Feeling sad, or what we may call 'depressed', happens to all of us and the sensation passes after a while. However, people with clinical depression (also known as Major Depressive Disorder) find that their state interferes with daily life, functioning, relating and the ability to made decisions. In addition, there may be changes in appetite and in sleep patterns, as well as poor concentration. Chemical imbalance plays a significant part.

Bipolar disorder (previously manic depression): Everybody experiences mood shifts but with bipolar disorder these changes are more extreme, featuring periods of overactive, excited behaviour, known as mania, and deep depression. Between these severe highs and lows there can be times of stability. Bipolar is categorised into Bipolar I (more mania than depression), Bipolar II (more depression and less severe mania, called hypomania) and Cyclothymia (highs and lows not as extreme). Those most likely to self-harm are those with Bipolar II.

Eating disorders: Anorexia, Bulimia and Compulsive Eating are coping mechanisms, put into place consciously or subconsciously in response to emotional pain. The anorexic severely restricts intake, the bulimic binges and purges and the compulsive eater overeats. Many people go undiagnosed and have a mix of eating disorders, best described as Eating Disorders Not Otherwise Specified (EDNOS).[2]

Personality disorders: The word 'personality' refers to the pattern of thoughts, feelings and behaviour that determine our uniqueness. People with personality disorders tend to have a limited range of emotions, attitudes and behaviours with which to cope. There are ten recognised personality disorders, the most common one associated with self-harm being Borderline

Personality Disorder. To be diagnosed with Borderline Personality Disorder a person needs to have five or more of the following symptoms impacting everyday life:[3]

- emotions that are up and down (eg feeling confidence one day and despair another), with feelings of emptiness and often anger
- difficulty in making and maintaining relationships
- an unstable sense of identity, such as thinking differently about yourself depending on who you are with
- taking risks or doing things without thinking about the consequences
- self-harming or thinking about self-harming (eg cutting, overdosing, etc)
- fear of being abandoned, rejected or alone
- sometimes believing in things that are not real or true (delusions) or seeing or hearing things that are not really there (hallucinations)

Dissociative disorders: Dissociation is a mental process where a person disconnects from their thoughts, feelings, memories or sense of identity. We all do this when we daydream or lose time on the motorway, but some people do it as a coping mechanism to block out pain. Dissociative disorders occur when you have persistent and repeated episodes of dissociation. There are a number of dissociative disorders: Depersonalisation Disorder, Dissociative Amnesia, Dissociative Fugue, Dissociative Identity Disorder (DID) and Dissociative Disorders Not Otherwise Specified (DDNOS). Each can cause internal chaos and some, especially DID, result in a splitting of self into parts, where just one part may self-harm.

Post Traumatic Stress Disorder (PTSD): Psychological trauma, particularly where there is loss of control and disempowerment, may result in an acute stress reaction. For some people this leads to Post Traumatic Stress Disorder (PTSD), characterised by four primary symptoms. These are **intrusion** (recurrent recollections of the event), **numbing** (emotional distancing from surrounding people and events), **avoidance** (fear and avoidance behaviour) and **arousal** (an agitated state of constant wakefulness and alertness).[4]

Substance abuse: This includes the abuse of any drug (over-the-counter, prescription, or illegal, alcohol, caffeine and nicotine), ingested, inhaled or injected and used to change a person's psychological or physical state. Self-harm has similar effects to some drugs; and both substance abuse and self-harm have the potential to become highly addictive. Some people may self-harm whilst on drugs; others interchange their addictions, which can include eating disorders.

Lack of life skills

One of the key factors behind self-harm is a feeling of powerlessness, hence the need to take power over the body. It's not just what happens to us, such as trauma, which can engender feelings of powerlessness, but also not having the necessary skills to cope with life's challenges. The skills we need in order to cope well include:

Communication skills:

- Listening and talking well, keeping conversation equal and flowing
- Knowing how to communicate with a variety of people: different backgrounds, ages, etc
- Expressing thoughts, feelings, ideas, opinions, preferences, values and beliefs with integrity

Relational skills:
- getting along with other people
- being able to form friendships, alliances and social networks
- being able to understand other people's strengths/weaknesses and to respect individuality
- having empathy, consideration and compassion
- being able to recognise and set healthy boundaries

Self-awareness skills:
- understanding personality, gifts and potential
- having a sense of belonging, destiny and purpose
- cultivating and nourishing character and drawing on life experiences
- learning how to stay focused and dealing with challenges and opportunities wisely

Problem solving skills:
- thinking about problems in such a way as to be able to recognise and name them, trace the roots and explore solutions
- learning from mistakes
- making good decisions
- keeping commitments
- knowing how to compromise and respect different opinions (to live without black and white thinking)

PAUSE FOR THOUGHT
Which life skills do you think you may lack? Pick the one you want to work on first.

EXTERNAL PRESSURES

Echoes of the past

Unwelcome and painful past events can interfere in the present. The experience can range from an uncomfortable reminder to severe flashbacks. Anything can act as a trigger: the way a person is treated, particular atmospheres, attitudes, voices, scenes on the TV, etc. The following outline suggests how to cope with a flashback:

1. Tell yourself that you are having a flashback.
2. Remind yourself that the worst is over.
3. Get grounded (more about this later).
4. Breathe.
5. Reorient to the present.
6. Get in touch with your need for boundaries.
7. Get support.
8. Take the time to recover.
9. Honour your experience.
10. Be patient.

Changes in circumstances

Both trauma and emotional fragility (depression, bipolar, hormone imbalance, etc) often result in a person being more sensitive to change, which can be experienced as loss of control. The person who has a traumatic history battles with ongoing internal chaos and often functions in crisis mode, with the internal chaos being reflected on the outside. Regularity, predictability and consistency will help the person to feel safer internally.

INTERNAL BATTLES

Feelings and fears

There is a great deal occurring on the inside that maintains destructive patterns for the person who self-harms, such as feelings of failure, low self-worth and self-hatred. The person may also lack confidence; compare him/herself unfavourably to others; feel physically unattractive; fear people, rejection or the future, and feel guilt or shame.

Thoughts and beliefs

Behind negative feelings lie negative thoughts and for the person who self-harms these can be overwhelming, such as:

'I'm not as good as other people.'

'I don't belong.'

'I shouldn't have been born.'

'I never get anything right.'

'I'm dirty, bad, evil.'

'I mustn't ever feel anything bad.'

'I'm hopeless, worthless, a waste of space, etc.'

Looking at what else might be going on for the person besides the self-harming behaviour can be overwhelming, but it also offers hope. When a person is given a proper diagnosis it helps provide personal insight and the opportunity to seek appropriate treatment/support.

REFLECTION

We are all different! No one will have exactly the same story when it comes to what causes and perpetuates their self-harm. Try to accept who you are; self-acceptance is an integral part of healing.

ACTION

Think about and write down any other struggles you have that might be contributing to or meeting the same needs as the self-harm. Do these lead to unhelpful thoughts or feelings?

PRAYER

Dear God, please help me to read Your Word, believe the truth of who I am and know that You haven't forgotten me and will meet my needs. Amen.

CHAPTER 4

THE SELF-HARM CYCLE

REPEATING THE BEHAVIOUR

We've talked about the behaviour of self-harm but what is it that draws people to repeatedly injure themselves?

> Emily, aged 24, says
> 'I have to self-harm when life becomes too much, but it's more than that, I *plan* to self-harm too. I know that sounds terrible but I think about it and my heart races with both anticipation and excitement. It's as though something is drawing me to do it and I can't live without it. I suppose it's a bit like someone on drugs ... you know it's bad for you and yet you want it, need it, make space for it.'

For many people, self-harm is more than a behaviour that occurs on occasions in response to difficult feelings. It's a pattern, a learned style of coping, a dependency and an addiction. An addiction is a state of being enslaved to a habit or practice. Do you feel enslaved at times? Perhaps you feel that the need to self-harm controls you more than you control it? The slippery slope to an addiction begins with a thought or in some cases observing another person carrying out a similar act and wondering if it will also help you. Although, with hindsight, it's easier to see when the problem began, at the time it's almost impossible to foresee the dangers of what lies ahead and to comprehend the physical and psychological damage.

Jenny says
'My self-harm felt like a magnet pulling me. Sometimes the pull was so strong it was as if I had no choice but to injure myself. The trouble was, the more frequently I did it the more I needed to and each time what I was doing got that bit worse. Self-harming solved one problem and created another. At the time I felt like I would never break out of it.'

THE SELF-HARM CYCLE
To understand why the magnetic pull occurs it can be helpful to look at self-harm in terms of a cycle. On the next page is an outline of a cycle that can be adapted to fit a person's situation; you may want to add your own words to personalise it. The aim of the cycle is to help you not only understand what is driving your behaviour, but to be empowered to make different and healthier choices.

Inner pain

The self-harm cycle begins with painful inner emotions such as grief, sorrow, anger, anxiety, despair, guilt and shame. Life brings many upheavals and hurts along the way, and the personality of the self-harmer may increase the hurt, fears and disturbing thoughts. Added to this are the person's beliefs about whether they have power over a situation or are powerless, that is, can they bring about change and learn to cope by challenging their thinking and taking practical steps, or is their wellbeing entirely dependent on their circumstances and therefore outside of their control? This concept is referred to as 'locus of control'.

49

'Locus of control' in social psychology refers to the extent to which individuals believe that they can control the events that affect them. One's locus (Latin for 'place' or 'location') can either be internal or external. Individuals with a high internal locus of control believe that they control their lives and that events result primarily from their own behaviour and actions. Individuals with a high external locus of control believe that their environment or other people control their decisions and determine events.

Often without realising it, the self-harmer will remain in situations where they will encounter additional stress and feel powerless to change their own circumstances, purely because it is what they are used to. 'Locus of control' is largely shaped by events in childhood that lead a person either to a position of 'empowerment' or of 'learned helplessness'. When the person discovers that happiness does lie within the way they perceive and manage situations, it becomes possible to shift the 'locus of control' towards that which brings freedom.

Emotional overload
With high levels of inner pain already in existence and an external 'locus of control' in operation, the self-harmer can find themselves experiencing emotional overload all too quickly – it doesn't take much additional stress to 'tip them over'. They may not understand what is happening but emotions and stress build up to such an extent that feelings become unbearable and impossible to contain. Suddenly the person reaches the point of feeling 'I can't cope'.

A helpful analogy is to view your emotional life as two buckets: one for positive emotions and one for negative emotions.

Without necessarily being aware of it, most of us keep our buckets balanced. An event or thought may occur which brings uncomfortable or painful feelings, which, if we are healthy, we acknowledge. If it is not an appropriate time to deal with it, we draw on inner resources and positive experiences to shift our focus, lessen the pain and return to a state of equilibrium. However, because people who self-harm don't know how to deal with adverse emotions, their negative buckets fill very quickly. In addition their positive buckets are naturally low due to a history of stress, trauma and depression. Self-harm becomes a way in which the sufferer can empty the negative bucket effectively.

Mel says
'The best way I can describe things is that my head would often feel full: full of pain, noise, demands, memories and thoughts. It was hard enough trying to get through the day but if any extra stress got thrown my way or people said upsetting words I would go into emotional overload in a split second. One minute I was coping, the next minute I'd be in meltdown and desperate to do something destructive to myself.'

Trigger
Living under a cloud of stored up negative emotions and other internal stresses leaves the self-harmer in a precarious state. Possible triggers include:
- loss of any kind
- flashbacks
- being shouted at

- being in a controlling environment
- being left out or ignored
- seeing operations, blood, etc
- stress
- painful memories
- arguments
- change of routine
- particular movies
- separations and goodbyes
- feeling lonely
- feeling invisible or small
- particular smells, music, places, etc

Ruth says
   'Some of my triggers were small, like feeling someone had rejected me, looked at me the wrong way, or I had been unable to complete a task. Soon there were triggers everywhere. I just couldn't get through the day without hurting myself.'

Triggers can take you back into the past and leave you feeling disorientated. To help reduce the power of triggers try using the following grounding skills, beneficial in managing overwhelming feelings and intense anxiety. They will also help to re-orientate you in the here-and-now.
- keep your eyes open, look around the room, notice your surroundings
- breathe deeply and slowly

- remind yourself what year it is … say it out loud
- put your feet firmly on the ground and touch something near you
- hold a pillow, stuffed animal or a ball
- focus on someone's voice or a neutral conversation
- place a cool cloth on your face, or hold something cold such as a can of drink

Alternatively, you could use the 54321 exercise, in which you name:

5 things you can *see* in the room (picture, plant)

4 things you can *feel* ('back of chair' or 'feet on floor')

3 things you can *hear* (cars, TV, birds)

2 things you can *smell* (that you like)

1 *good* thing about yourself

Self-harm act

The person who self-harms becomes desperate for release from the intense build-up inside their mind, a bit like a fizzy drink bottle shaken to the point of explosion. The sequence of events that follow the trigger feels inevitable: something must happen to reduce the intensity of pain. Self-harming breaks the power of the inner torture, whereby the emotional pain is expressed in a physical manner. The pain becomes visible, tangible, explainable and treatable.

Kate says

'It was a quick, easy way to cope with very intense negative emotions like feelings of loss, lack of control, fear, and anger ... in my mind it was a lot like the use of cowpox to prevent smallpox (if exposed to the first one, you were unlikely to get the second). In my mind, if I cut I'd never feel the full blown effect of emotional pain.'

Ruth says

'I would often feel like I was on a rollercoaster and I just needed to get off. Hurting myself and then being cared for at the hospital was a way of getting off the rollercoaster momentarily.'

Mel says

'Part of me was overcome by emotional pain and crying out to get rid of it and another part of me felt the adrenalin pumping around my body and excited at the thought of what I knew I would end up doing. It was almost as though I enjoyed the ritual of cutting.'

For some the act is fast, over in seconds; for others the whole process is slow, drawn out, concentrated, ritualistic.

Temporary relief

When people who self-harm get emotionally overwhelmed, the act of self-harm brings their levels of psychological and physiological tension and arousal back to a bearable level almost immediately. It's like the calm after the storm. The emotional pain seems to fade away as the intensity of the physical sensation takes over. The biology of this is explained in Chapter 2 where we looked at how the release of neurochemicals (endorphins) when self-harming create heightened feelings of pleasure, well-being and numbness to pain resulting in a temporarily reduction or removal of emotional turmoil. That's why self-harm becomes so addictive: it's an instant solution to pain.

The trouble is that this method of dealing with pain is, as it suggests, *temporary*. It does not solve the problem; it merely masks it with 'high' feelings. When those feelings dissipate, the person is back in a place of negative thoughts and overwhelming emotions, once more feeding the cycle.

PAUSE FOR THOUGHT

People who self-harm often talk about how difficult it is to stop because the urges are so strong. Is this your experience? Do you have uncomfortable physical feelings when you try to stop, such as agitation, aches and shakiness?

If you are wondering whether you are dependent on self-harm, ask yourself the following questions:

Do I think about self-harm most days?

Do I plan when and where I will self-harm?

Do I find my eyes drawn to items in a room with which I could self-harm?

Do I 'dream' about the times I have harmed myself?

Do I wonder what the next self-harm act will be like?

Do I find that I say I am going to stop, but then do it again?

Do I hurt myself more often than I once did?

Do I need to hurt myself more severely than I used to?

Do I feel tense, anxious, stressed or agitated when not able to self-harm?

Do I have a sense of urgency about needing to self-harm?

Has self-harm become my main way of coping?

If you found yourself answering 'yes' to most of the questions, it may be beneficial to seek professional help.

Guilt and shame

If self-harm truly worked as a way of dealing with internal and external stress the relief felt would last and the cycle would end. However, the relief experienced is counterfeit because something deeper is going on at the core of the cycle. Two emotions are most likely driving the cycle. Guilt says: 'I've done something wrong'. Shame says: 'There's something profoundly wrong with me'.

Guilt tends to kick-start the cycle, whereas shame is there in the background, keeping the cycle alive. Jerusha Clarke says, 'Insidiously, shame tells self-injurers that they are unworthy of grace, of the freedom and lightness they crave.'[1] Most people who self-harm hold very powerful beliefs about being flawed, not good enough, being bad or being responsible for the painful events that have occurred in their lives, and, without realising it, wear a cloak of shame. Whilst the physical release of harming yourself brings an altered state of mood and a completion of the cycle, the shame sits festering, waiting for another incident involving powerful emotions like guilt and anger to set the cycle going again.

In Chapter 8 we will look at the importance of understanding our true value as a person and healing from the negative thoughts and experiences that cause shame to take such a hold.

REFLECTION

Many people feel enslaved by their self-harm, and feel that it controls them rather than them controlling it. But the more we let Jesus into our lives and allow Him to share our struggles, the greater our sense of control.

ACTION

Draw your own version of the self-harm cycle (or a version for someone you know who is struggling). Instead of our words, add in words that are specific to your experience. Can you see how the cycle works in your life?

PRAYER

Dear God, in Galatians 5:1, Your word says that we don't have to be slaves any more and 2 Timothy 1:7 says that Your Spirit gives us power, love and self-discipline. Please help me to be set free from any kind of emotional slavery. Amen.

PART 2:
THE PATH TO RECOVERY

CHAPTER 5

FIRST STEPS

ONE STEP AT A TIME

It's hard to admit the full extent of any problem, and when you finally do there can be an overwhelming sense of 'this is too big to face'. Perhaps you feel like that now or have done so in the past. It may be difficult to know how to go about dealing with your self-harm, so we have broken it down into four stages:

Stage 1: breaking the secrecy

Stage 2: contemplating the pros and cons

Stage 3: making the decision to stop

Stage 4: seeking help and support

STAGE 1: BREAKING THE SECRECY

To overcome self-harm you will need to face the truth that you are a self-harmer and take the brave step of confiding in someone. When you confide you are entrusting what you share to another person and allowing them to help carry the weight of the burden.

Lucy says

'There are people who will never understand why some people are driven to hurt themselves, but there are others who will love you despite what you are going through. Surround yourself with people who will support you, and get counselling if you can. Being able to talk with somebody who isn't emotionally involved can be very helpful.'

Self-harm has a hold because it is both secretive and addictive, and these feed off each other. The thought of talking to someone can be pretty frightening, but as long as you live with the secrecy it continues to have power over you. You may have already told someone that you self-harm without necessarily being completely open about what you do, how often and how you feel. On the other hand you may have been honest and the other person didn't take it well. Finding the right person is key. It needs to be someone who is non-judgmental, who will listen and keep confidences, has life experience, including some understanding of addictive patterns, and who also has godly wisdom.

You will probably have worked extremely hard to hide the self-harm, so talking to someone in an open manner can feel like a betrayal, as though you are letting yourself down. You may think it weak and shameful, but it's not a sign of weakness at all. You may find it hard to know what to say at first and stumble over communicating, but that's OK. Helpguide offers some useful information on how to talk.[1]

Tips for talking about cutting and self-harm

Focus on your feelings: Instead of sharing sensational details of your self-harm behaviour – what specifically you do to hurt yourself – focus on the feelings or situations that lead to it. This can help the person you're confiding in to better understand where you're coming from. It also helps to let the person know why you're telling them. Do you want help or advice from them? Do you simply want another person to know so you can let go of the secret?

Communicate in whatever way you feel most comfortable: If you're too nervous to talk in person, consider starting off the conversation with an email or letter (although it's important to eventually follow up with a face-to-face conversation). Don't feel pressured into sharing things you're not ready to talk about. You don't have to show the person your injuries or answer any questions you don't feel comfortable answering.

Give the person time to process what you tell them: As difficult as it is for you to open up, it may also be difficult for the person you tell – especially if it's a close friend or family member. Sometimes, you may not like the way the person reacts. Try to remember that reactions such as shock, anger, and fear come out of concern for you. It may help to show these tips to the people you choose to tell. The better they understand self-harm, the better they will be able to support you.

Talking about self-harm can be very stressful and bring up a lot of emotions. Don't be discouraged if the situation feels worse for a short time right after sharing your secret. It's uncomfortable to confront and change long-standing habits, but once you get past these initial challenges you'll start to feel better.

STAGE 2: CONTEMPLATING THE PROS AND CONS

Recognising ambivalence

Ambivalence means being torn between two options, and is a word that, for some, very accurately describes the feelings surrounding wanting, and yet fearing, recovery. Perhaps you feel you desperately want to be rid of self-harm but also feel paralysed by the fear of how you will live without it.

> Babs says
>
> 'I longed to be free from self-harm but I didn't want to give up the relief it brought me. I only wanted to stop self-harming if I could guarantee never feeling bad in life and having the same buzz it gave me. Of course I came to realise that this was completely unrealistic and I would have to take the risk of what life was going to be like without it. Now I can honestly say that life without self-harm is so much better. Yes, life has its ups and downs but it feels so good to respond to these without self-harming. I feel stronger, more in control and I respect myself much more.'

It's helpful to look at the advantages and disadvantages of self-harm. Many have seen it as both their best friend and their worst enemy. Below is a suggested exercise. Use the columns to add in your pros and cons and give each pointer a score of 1–10 (1 = least significant and 10 = most significant). Count up how many points you have in each column.

Advantages: a method of dealing with difficult emotions and trauma, etc. Disadvantages: secrecy, pain, feeling trapped, etc.

Advantages to self-harming	1-10	Disadvantages to self-harming	1-10
Example: It temporarily brings an end to emotional pain	8	Example: I never learn how to process emotions	9
Example: It is a good way to punish myself	6	Example: It leaves me feeling very guilty	7

When your list of disadvantages outweighs the advantages, you are in a much stronger place to recover. But don't worry, if the advantages exceed the disadvantages, you can still work at getting better; you may just find yourself slipping back a little more frequently. Whatever the situation, focus on the positives of life without self-harm and all the ways it holds you back.

PAUSE FOR THOUGHT

Ask yourself a few honest questions and write the answers in your notebook. (Do I want to stop self-harming? Even if I'm fearful or have mixed feelings, am I willing to give it a go? Can I accept that sometimes it's going to go well and other times not so well?)

STAGE 3: MAKING THE DECISION TO STOP

Why stop?

Why stop when something works? It's a good question to ask. Self-harm may dissolve tension and anger but is replaced by shame and self-loathing. Keeping up the secrecy of self-harm is also isolating and results in the loss of meaningful friendships. People begin to see you as unfriendly, not interested, and secretive; misunderstandings and defence barriers build up.

> Gemma says
>
> 'Eventually I saw that cutting didn't actually help me deal with the issues that made me want to hurt myself in the first place and that self-harm was a barrier to living a full and fulfilled life.'

Stepping out

For any one of us, following through on change can be equally as hard, if not harder, than making the initial decision. How many times have you said to yourself, 'I'm not going to do this again' and then along comes a trigger or stressful situation, even boredom or loneliness, and you find yourself on the downward spiral? You may even wonder if there really is life beyond self-harming and if so whether it is genuinely better.

Louise says

'When I felt an emotion I felt overwhelmed. Cutting blocked that off so I learnt not to feel. Even happy emotions were off the agenda in case they were taken away from me or changed into sadness and anger. As I began to recover I discovered that it was OK to feel. It didn't last and was like a wave that reached a peak and came down again.

'To begin with, life without cutting felt much worse, but as I felt safe and loved and allowed myself to receive God's love I started to feel free. The urge to cut became less frequent. Counselling, prayer, attending Christian retreats and specific courses on overcoming self-harm and eating disorders all played an important part in my recovery.

'I've not cut now for two years and I can honestly say I don't want to. There are times when that voice in my head says, "Cut, go on, you will feel better," but I am now much more able to say *"STOP! What do I need right now that is making me think about cutting?"* People used to say to me, "You have a choice," which made me feel so angry. Although now I can see where they were coming from, at the time I didn't believe I could make a positive choice. What I needed was for people to help demonstrate the kind of choices available and offer to work with me. I now feel empowered, renewed, hopeful and free to be the person God wants me to be.'

Louise admits that she wouldn't be where she is today had she not had good support and sought professional help.

STAGE 4: SEEKING HELP AND SUPPORT

Whether or not you have been able to open up to someone close, it's important to pursue professional help to oversee your care and progress. Of course, it is possible to recover without such help, but you may find yourself in a much more vulnerable position.

GP: Your GP will check your overall health (sometimes self-harm can result in health problems such as low blood count). He or she will also check your mental health and, if needed, prescribe medication (anti-depressants or anti-anxiety drugs) and/or make a referral to a psychiatrist, NHS counsellor, cognitive behavioural or other therapist, or for inpatient help. Depending on where you live (hence which Trust you come under), you may also be put in touch with the Community Mental Health Team (CMHT) and be given a care co-ordinator to help work with you to monitor change.

Inpatient treatment: This may be a spell in a psychiatric hospital if the self-harming is particularly bad, there are concerns over other diagnoses, or it is necessary for you to have a supervised medication change. Another option might be to receive help in a private clinic that treats life-controlling addictions. Your GP should know what is available and if funding is possible.

Counselling and psychotherapy: Counselling and psychotherapy are umbrella terms that cover a range of talking therapies. They are delivered by trained practitioners who work in the short- or long-term with people to help them bring about effective change or enhance their wellbeing.[2] The actual word 'psychotherapy' comes from the ancient Greek word 'psyche', meaning breath, spirit or soul. The word 'therapy' means to nurse or cure. A psychotherapist helps you to make sense of your self-harming and what role it plays by identifying causes and enabling you to re-evaluate the way you see yourself. Some therapists are trained to use art, music, drama, dance or other creative tools in addition to talking.

REFLECTION
Breaking secrecy is important because things kept secret have power over us. Sometimes it does feel worse before it feels better, but secrecy has a huge cost, and openness leads to long-term freedom.

ACTION
If you've never confided in anyone about your self-harm, decide whom you could tell based on the list above, and write his or her name in your notebook, along with some thoughts about what you might want to say. If you've already done this, write down some ideas of help and support you could get, based on the fourth stage.

PRAYER
Dear God, please give me the courage to share my self-harming with people who can help and support me. Please would You give me the words to say and help me to see the choices You give me. Amen.

CHAPTER 6

SETTING GOALS

RECOVERY PLAN

Have you ever tried to set out on a journey without a plan of how you intend to get there or the necessities for the trip? It could be interesting! Some people have done just that and still arrived at their destination, but they probably experienced a few diversions. Establishing a plan for recovery involves giving foresight to the way forward.

In the Introduction we suggested you buy a large notebook with dividers where you can store all the information aimed at helping you to recover. The following are some of the areas you may like to consider as a part of your 'recovery book'.

Goal setting: a plan of your goals and what you need to achieve them

Contacts: organisations, helplines, or people who have agreed to support you

Resources: details of any recommended reading or good websites

Encouragement: scriptures, sayings, or affirming words given by other people

Prayers: write out your own prayers or copy them from books or the internet and pray each day

Causes and triggers: keep adding anything which comes to mind that is behind your self-harm

Feelings: make a note of your feelings, especially around the time you self-harm (or want to)

Negative thoughts: what negative thoughts might lie behind your feelings?

Distractions: anything beneficial that will take your focus away from self-harming

This is by no means an exhaustive list, but it's a good place to start. Let's look at each of these in a little more detail.

GOAL SETTING

What are your goals in relation to recovery? Are some more of a priority than others? It's useful to consider short and long-term goals. For instance, a short-term goal might be to use distractions to help prevent the self-harm, whilst a long-term goal could be to stop self-harming.

You may find yourself being idealistic: setting very high goals and then condemning yourself when you don't achieve them. It's important to set manageable goals which will propel you forward in your recovery rather than disappoint you and cause you to give up. Understanding SMART goals[1] can help. Goals should be straightforward and emphasise what you want to happen. Goal objectives should address the five W's: who, what, when, where, and why. Use action words such as: create, develop, direct, implement, organise, establish, plan, etc.

The SMART goal concept was originally designed for use in the Business and Management world to help set goals that encourage rather than frustrate. Each letter of the word SMART stands for an element that needs to be considered:

Specific
Measurable
Attainable
Relevant
Time-bound

Specific: Your goal needs to state specifically *what* you want to accomplish. When goals are specific it helps us to focus our efforts and clearly define what we are going to do. Example:

Nonspecific: 'My goal is to get better.'

Specific: 'My goal is to not self-harm for a week and to phone someone if I am struggling.'

Measurable: A measurable goal helps you to see change occur by asking the question: How much do I want to achieve right now? When you can measure your progress you are more likely to stay on track and be encouraged, which, in turn, spurs you on to continue reaching this and other goals. Example:

Non Measurable: 'My goal is to stop self-harming.'

Measurable: 'My goal is to reduce my self-harming from every day to three times a week.'

Attainable: Your goal needs to stretch you, but still be realistic. There needs to be a degree of hard work in order to grow and attain a sense of achievement. Try to identify goals that are particularly important to you, since you will be more motivated to work at these. Example:

Non Attainable: 'My goal is to stop self-harming.'

Attainable: 'My goal is to avoid self-harm by using my alternative strategies, and if I cut to use a clean blade.'

Relevant: A relevant goal takes into consideration the current conditions and realities of your personal situation. Setting a goal that is relevant to your life now will encourage you to work towards it. This means looking at the appropriateness of the goal you are setting in conjunction with your current circumstances. Example:

Non Relevant: 'My goal is to stop self-harming.'

Relevant: 'During this period of exams I know it isn't going to work to stop cutting but I want to reduce the severity of it, so that I will have made some progress. After the exams I will concentrate on working towards not cutting.

Time-bound: A time-bound goal states when you want to accomplish something by, or where you want to be in one, two or six weeks from now. Making goals time-bound means giving them a target date. A commitment to a deadline helps you focus your efforts on completing your goal, for instance:

Non Time-bound: 'My goal is to stop self-harming.'

Time-bound: 'In one week I want to have reduced the severity of my injuries. In six weeks I want to have reduced my incidents of self-harm and by the time I go on holiday I want to have stopped self-harming.'

Goals are fluid: there is nothing to say that your goals can't change as you go through the process. For example if you feel that your progress is being too rushed, re-assess the 'Time-bound' area. If you aren't sure if you're achieving what you set out to do, look at the 'Specific' area and if you aren't making progress, look at the 'Attainable' area. As you complete your goals you can add new ones into your recovery plan.

CONTACTS

It is extremely useful to create a list of helpful contacts in your notebook so that they are readily available. You may also want to store them on your phone or on a piece of paper that you carry around with you. This could include your GP or NHS 111 (previously NHS Direct). It could also include your vicar, pastor, youth leader or church pastoral team, a counsellor, a therapist or a friend.

Remember that each person is only a link. The two most important people in your recovery are you and God. Others are there to help you to take *your own* steps, not to rescue you. If you look to them for the answers, you will not only find yourself let down, misunderstood and hurt at times (no one is perfect), you will also run the risk of relying on others for your affirmation, depriving yourself of the vital life skill of self-affirmation (helping yourself in the midst of difficulty).

When you have identified people, clarify with each individual the role they are willing to play and set some boundaries together, looking at what is reasonable contact. This may sound hard, but many people have been hurt in the care they receive because both parties have different expectations. When someone is hurting, they can put pressure on people without meaning to, so it is important to set and respect boundaries. The end result will be more rewarding.

RESOURCES

Aim to create your own list of organisations, useful websites and books. The following are a few ideas (there are additional ones in the resources section at the end of the book):

Books
- *Secret Scars*, Abigail Robson, Authentic Media
- *Inside a Cutter's Mind*, Jerusha Clark and Dr Earl Henslin, NavPress
- *Crying Scarlet Tears*, Sophie Scott, Monarch Books

Websites
- Adullam Ministries: www.adullam-ministries.org.uk
- National Self-harm Network: www.nshn.co.uk

Christian helplines
- Premier Lifeline: 0845 345 0707
- Crossline: 0300 111 0101
- UCB Prayerline: 0845 456 7729

Counselling
   To find a Christian counsellor in your area:
- ACC: www.acc-uk.org
- CWR: 01344 893197

ENCOURAGEMENT
It can be empowering to make your own list of scriptures, sayings and affirming words. The following are a start:
   Bible verses

Isaiah 41:10 'So do not fear, for I am with you; do not be dismayed, for I am your God. I will strengthen you and help you; I will uphold you with my righteous right hand.'

Jeremiah 29:11 '"For I know the plans I have for you," declares the LORD, "plans to prosper you and not to harm you, plans to give you hope and a future."'

Zephaniah 3:17 'The LORD your God is with you, he is Mighty to save. He will take great delight in you, he will quiet you with his love, he will rejoice over you with singing.'

Quotations

Max Lucado: 'You are valuable because you exist. Not because of what you do or what you have done, but simply because you are.'

Eve Sharon Hart: 'A successful life comes not from eliminating self-doubt but from accepting it and then pursuing your dreams anyway.'

Franklin D. Roosevelt: 'When you come to the end of your rope, tie a knot and hang on.'

Henry Ford: 'When everything seems to be going against you, remember that the airplane takes off against the wind, not with it.'

PRAYERS

What prayers have you read or heard people say which really spoke to you? It's good to write them down. Try to have a selection of different types of prayers, including thanksgiving, repentance, protection, help and warfare. *New Prayers*, by Michel Quoist and *10 Prayers You Can't Live Without*, by Rick Hamlin might be useful in helping you to know how to pray in different situations.

CAUSES AND TRIGGERS

Becoming aware of what triggers your self-harm and the different events in life that may have contributed to it becoming your way of coping, will, inevitably, be a gradual process. When something comes to mind about a possible cause or trigger jot it down in your recovery book so that you don't forget. You can explore its connection to your self-harm later or talk it through with your counsellor or whoever else is helping you. In Chapter 4 we looked at potential triggers so it might be useful to go back and reread the section. What situations trigger you the most? Are you more affected by environment, words, reminders of the past, changes in circumstances, let downs or rejection? As you add more situations in your recovery book, see if you can recognise a common theme developing; this will tell you about key areas in your life that need addressing.

FEELINGS

Feelings are often blocked off or experienced to an extreme. On the next page is a chart to help you to make a note of your feelings, especially around the time you self-harm/want to self-harm.

Alienated	Stubborn	Unhappy	Indifferent
Grumpy	Abused	Annoyed	At ease
Vulnerable	Degraded	Disgusted	Inadequate
Discounted	Anxious	Moody	Guilty
Bored	Ashamed	Brave	Concerned
Fearful	Bad	Compelled	Kind
Controlled	Abandoned	Angry	Loved
Driven	Dreadful	Rebellious	Mixed up
Dependent	Determined	Self-conscious	Worthless
Dissatisfied	Negative	Embarrassed	Apprehensive
Envious	Peaceful	Exhausted	Tense
Independent	Excited	Frustrated	Stupid
Uncomfortable	Fed up	Worried	Trapped
Hopeless	Lonely	Harassed	Hurt
Wanted	Miserable	Threatened	Rejected
Hopeful	Hated	Torn	Inhibited
Resentful	Impatient	Indignant	Scared
Unimportant	Childish	Helpless	Unloved
Unwanted	Liked	Humiliated	Shy
Reluctant	Patient	Unpopular	Puzzled
Paranoid	Relaxed	Secure	Timid
Tender	Terrified	Sad	Unsure

NEGATIVE THOUGHTS

As you will go on to see in Chapter 8, there is a strong connection between negative thoughts and feelings. To help work through these draw up three columns in your recovery book, as per the table on the next page. Each time you find yourself pulled down by an emotion identify it, write it down and work out what you may have been thinking which led to the emotion. If you can, try to challenge the thought.

Feeling	Thought	Challenge
Failure	I can't ever get anything right	I sometimes get things wrong but not always
Inferiority	I'm not as acceptable as others	I am as equal as anyone else even if I don't feel it
Shame	I'm bad inside	Bad things might have happened but I am not bad
Worthlessness	What I think or say doesn't count	My thoughts and options are just as valid as anyone else's
Anxiety	People won't understand	People may need my help to understand
Hopelessness	I can't get out of this mess	With the right help and taking one step at a time I can
Rejection	I'm not liked	There may be people who don't like me and those I don't like, but it isn't everyone

DISTRACTIONS

Distractions don't resolve the issues but can prevent you acting on impulse. It can often be useful to do something constructive with your hands to keep them occupied, such as using:

Thinking putty: which has a mind of its own and takes the shape of what it's in or on (www.puttyworld.co.uk).

A scratch map: take a coin and scratch off the foil to reveal a whole new, colourful world underneath (www.scratchmap.co.uk).

A doodle tablecloth: tablecloth that resembles a large sheet of wipeable graph paper, complete with a set of washable markers (www.amazon.co.uk).

Colouring books: there are a variety available for grown ups and young people. Great distraction!

Smiley bendy men: happy chaps that bend, stretch and are tactile (www.stresscheck.co.uk).

Aroma dough: an energising and stress relieving aid, with especially designed dough, infused with essential oils (www.sensorytoywarehouse.com).

Tangles: series of 90-degree curves, connected and able to pivot at each joint (www.sensorytoywarehouse.com).

HelpGuide[2] offers the following useful suggestions if you cut:

express pain and intense emotions: paint, draw, or scribble on a big piece of paper with red ink or paint. Express your feelings in a journal, compose a poem or song to say what you feel, write down any negative feelings and then rip the paper up or listen to music that expresses what you're feeling.

calm and soothe yourself: take a bath or hot shower. Pet or cuddle a dog or cat, wrap yourself in a warm blanket, massage your neck, hands, and feet or listen to calming music.

because you feel disconnected and numb: call a friend – you don't have to talk about self-harm. Take a cold shower, hold an ice cube in the crook of your arm or leg, chew something with a very strong taste, like chilli peppers, peppermint, or a grapefruit peel or go online to a self-help website, chat room, or message board.

to release tension or vent anger: exercise vigorously – run, dance, jump rope, or hit a punching bag. Punch a cushion or mattress or scream into your pillow, squeeze a stress ball or squish Play-Doh® or clay, rip something up (sheets of paper or a magazine) or make some noise (play an instrument or bang on pots and pans).

If any of the above distractions or alternatives jump out at you, or you have ideas that aren't listed, write them in your notebook for use when you need them.

REFLECTION

The thought of recovery may be overwhelming, but remember that by using just one of the suggestions in this chapter you are moving in the direction of freedom.

ACTION

Try to set your own SMART goal and write it down so that you can mark your progress. It doesn't matter if it doesn't work too well the first time round. Practice makes perfect!

PRAYER

Dear God, Your Word in Jeremiah 29:11 says that Your plans are not meant to harm me but that You intend for me to have a hope and a future. Thank You for the provision of all the tools in this chapter; may they offer me hope in the ups and downs. Amen.

CHAPTER 7

MAKING CHANGES

THOROUGH APPROACH

At the beginning of Chapter 3 we mentioned that self-harm is actually a solution, not the problem, so recovery will involve dealing with the causes of the self-harm, not just the behaviour.

In the midst of struggling with self-harm, Louise created an acronym.

Secrets
Empty
Lonely
Frightened
Hateful
Alienated
Rejected
Misunderstood

Perhaps you can relate to what she wrote. For as long as

these words dominated her life she was caught in a web of pain and self-loathing – the self-harm cycle. Her recovery involved dealing with the five areas that make up human functioning: physical, emotional, volitional, rational and spiritual.

With each of the five areas of human functioning there are negative and positive aspects. The first draws you into the self-harm cycle, the second works to break it.

Physical: harm vs nurture

Emotional: suppression vs expression

Volitional: powerlessness vs choice

Rational: misbelief vs truth

Spiritual: self-rejection vs self-worth

We are going to explore the physical and emotional areas in this chapter, and the volitional, rational and spiritual in Chapter 8.

PHYSICAL: HARM VS NURTURE

Negative	Positive
Not looking after wounds	Cleaning wounds and receiving correct treatment
Hating and giving no regard to your body	Learning to accept your body
Not caring about the long term effects	Helping your body to heal
Depriving yourself	Nurturing yourself

What needs to change physically isn't just the actual act of harming yourself, but the way you view and treat your body as a whole. It's too easy to separate your body from the rest of you and hence have little regard for what you do to it, which may include changing your diet and creating a right sleep routine, as well as dealing with the more obvious self-harm.

The reasons people have for harming themselves tend to be

related to unprocessed emotional wounds in childhood. When you hurt your body, it is as though you are hurting the child inside. Your body pays the price it shouldn't have to pay. If you can, try to be aware of the hurt child and ask yourself, 'If this was someone else's child would I hurt her or him?' Then you may find it easier to resist inflicting wounds on yourself.

It's also important to recognise that you are made in the image of God – read Genesis 1:27 – that He chose you – Ephesians 1:4 – and that you are fearfully and wonderfully made – Psalm 139:14. When you value yourself as God's child it becomes harder to damage that creation. We will explore this more in Chapter 8.

Learning to care for your body

Reaching the stage of caring for your body to the extent that you don't harm it is a process which takes time. To assist the process and prevent more damage, try:

Using safe methods: if you self-harm make sure that the implements are clean.

Looking after wounds: cuts and burns can become infected, so it's important to keep them clean.

Helping scars heal: there are creams and oils you can buy which help to improve the appearance of new and old scars.

You can also care for your body by:

Maintaining medication: to avoid sudden changes in mood (always talk to your GP before changing or stopping any medication).

Eating regular meals: to avoid dips in blood sugar resulting in you becoming reactive/impulsive.

Keeping alcohol to a minimum: to avoid becoming emotional and out of control.

Living with scars

Living free from self-harm also means learning to live with some of the consequences, such as scars. It's worth remembering that everyone has scars of some sort, but most are emotional scars, not scars as visible as those caused by self-harm. Most of the time people are just curious and might not even connect your scars with self-harm. Preparing yourself with answers should anyone question you can be helpful. The following are a few ideas of how to respond when asked about scars.

'Self-harm is something I'm still really struggling with, but I'm getting help with it and hope to recover soon.'

'I had a problem with self-harm a few years ago, and I'm left with some of the scars, but I'm so much better on the inside.'

Children might seem the most curious, but they are often satisfied with the simplest explanations: 'It used to hurt, but it doesn't any more.'

It's always OK to say if you don't want to talk about it, but you don't have to get defensive. People will normally accept it if you say 'I'm not comfortable talking about it at the moment,' especially if you can add, 'Can we talk about it another time?' or, 'I can recommend a book if you are interested in the issue?'

Lucy says

'It has been years since I last cut myself. My scars have now faded to white (from pink/purple), but still remain and are visible when wearing short sleeves. Sometimes they really bother me as they remind me of bad times and how depressed I was, but they also show me how far I have come. I have survived and, like it or not, my scars are a part of who I am.'

EMOTIONAL: SUPPRESSION VS EXPRESSION

Negative	Positive
Fear and avoidance of difficult emotions	Being brave enough to learn about difficult emotions
Blurring all uncomfortable feelings into one	Learning to identify and name feelings
Thinking that the feeling will go on forever	Reminding yourself that even horrible feelings do end
Hating the child inside, punishing/lashing out	Nurturing the child so she/he can heal and grow up
Self-harming to get rid of 'bad' emotions	Learning to process emotions without self-harm

Emotions are a part of life and we all have them – good, bad or indifferent. Negative emotions, although unpleasant, are important because they are signposts that indicate something needs addressing. When we have a healthy relationship with ourselves, others and God, we not only take notice of our emotions but we largely respond to, and process, them in constructive ways. However, when we don't have a healthy relationship with them they become out of perspective, out of control or greatly feared. Dealing with emotions is normally something we learn as we are growing up, modelled by our parents and other significant adults.

PAUSE FOR THOUGHT

How did/do those close to you manage their emotions? In what way has this had an impact on you?

One step at a time

There are two stages in dealing with emotions:

Recognising: which we considered in Chapter 6 (look back at the list of feelings).

Responding: working to prevent emotions from building up and controlling your life; expressing them in a healthy, non-destructive, way.

Emotions that are turned inwards and suppressed become toxic, festering away inside; emotions that are turned outwards and expressed without appropriate understanding and control can be equally damaging. It may be useful to think about formulating a way to express emotions; this might feel a bit contrived but will help prevent you automatically going down the self-harm route.

- talk to safe people about how you feel
- practice being honest about feeling bad before it becomes unbearable
- draw an angry picture (red is a good colour)
- if the emotion becomes too strong turn the paper over and draw a sad picture as this dilutes the anger because you are getting in touch with the opposite emotion
- do the same as above for when you feel sad (draw an angry picture to dilute the sadness)
- go for a fast walk (this can calm you down)
- write in your recovery book (look at the ideas mentioned in Chapter 6)
- pray and read the Psalms (the psalmist knew how to express his feelings)
- do something you enjoy to help produce positive feelings and counteract negative ones

- release endorphins through:
  - exercising (find a form that best suits you)
  - smiling (practise smiling at people)
  - laughing (watch a good film)
  - having fun (be a little daft)
  - eating dark chocolate (in moderation)
  - eating spicy food
  - listening to music
  - being out in the countryside using your senses
  - spending time in the sun

An important aspect of dealing with unpleasant emotions is learning to sit with them rather than run away from them. Practise sitting with emotions – put off self-harming for a few minutes, then for a few more. Take comfort from the fact that emotions are like a wave – they build up and up, but by the law of gravity must come down. With self-harm you short circuit the emotion rather than ride the wave and never learn that you can survive and come out stronger.

Emotional buttons
When you have been through difficult experiences and they remain unhealed, it is easy for your 'emotional buttons' to get pressed. For instance if you were bullied or left out of activities at school, when someone in the here-and-now leaves you out or appears not to talk to you whilst still engaging with others, it can press the old pain buttons, sometimes spoken of as triggers.

Some triggers can be dealt with by completely avoiding a situation or person; some can't. However, you can learn to deal with them to lessen the intensity. For example, if you know that passing by the shop where you used to buy razor blades triggers negative feelings, avoid that shop. If you are elsewhere and unexpectedly see the same blades you will need to have strategies in place.

Learning to separate the past from the present is vital. When faced with a situation that presses buttons, the tendency is to experience the emotions that belonged to a stressful or traumatic event in the past as though occurring at this moment in time. You need to remind the wounded child inside that the feelings were then and *it is different now*. You have resources available to you now as an adult that you didn't have when you were younger.

> Jenny says
> 'A trigger for me was seeing men with beards, because when I was abused I could always see and feel the abuser's beard against my face. I couldn't avoid beards forever, so I had to learn to deal with them. Beards still remind me of the abuse, but I don't feel like I'm re-experiencing it any more.'

Jenny went through a desensitising process which involved talking about beards with a counsellor or trusted friend; looking at pictures of men with beards and watching a TV programme including a bearded man. She also sat in a shopping precinct watching people, including men with beards, and found someone she trusted who had a beard and who was happy to let her feel it.

Through this process, as well as receiving prayer and counselling, Jenny was able to come to the place where men with beards no longer posed a threat.

Healing from painful experiences

To begin to move away from self-harm it is essential to find healing from past hurts. As we said earlier, there is often a wounded child inside a grownup who has gone through childhood trauma or whose needs were not met. The person gets stuck emotionally at the age she/he was wounded. Do you feel that's true for you? The 'child' only heals as she/he receives what was needed when younger, and you are the only one who can give that to her/him. Love, nurture, affirmation, and being heard and cared for are crucial to the healing process. Can you begin to respond towards yourself with a little more kindness and compassion? I (Helena) once wrote a poem that illustrates the necessity to heal from past hurts in order to overcome self-harm.

Frozen tears
Tears fall inside, forbidden and unseen;
only the little girl knows what they mean.
She's learned it's dangerous to express;
so the hurt inside she must repress:
the confusion, loneliness and fears
behind her many frozen tears.
No one notices that things aren't right
or asks what's happening out of sight.
No one utters the crucial line:
'I'd like to give you some of my time
to see a picture or hear a song
about a girl who feels so wrong.'
The years go by: the adult appears,
she too, is bound by frozen tears.
A cloud of depression covers her all:

she's empty, aching, and destined to fall
into some sort of pit or destructive form,
unable to face the turbulent storm.
Her head feels full and ready to crack
there are images, voices … the little girl's back.
She can no longer run from what's happening inside:
there's no place left on earth to hide
so she downs the pills and cuts her arm;
she wants it to end … means no harm.
Self-harm says she's alive, not frozen in ice
but her body bears the scar of every slice.
She's hated herself for too many years:
it's time to face the pain and feel those tears
which belong to a child who took the blame;
buried herself in a cloak of shame.

REFLECTION

You may not always have been treated kindly by other people or treated your body with respect. Today is a new day; a chance to become more compassionate towards yourself.

ACTION

Try writing an acronym for SELF HARM like Louise's at the beginning of the chapter. Focus on what self-harm means to you.

PRAYER

Dear God, You tell me that I am made in Your image, fearfully and wonderfully made and You rejoice over me with singing. Help me to treat myself as You, Jesus, treated people. Amen.

CHAPTER 8

HEALING THE HEART

FROM THE INSIDE OUT

Many people make the mistake of focusing too much on the outward actions of self-harm – the symptoms – and not enough on what is really happening in a person's inner world. A wounded heart often leads to a wounded body. Emotional and spiritual healing needs to take place from the inside out. There needs to be change in choices, thinking and self-worth (the volitional, rational and spiritual aspects of human functioning).

VOLITIONAL: POWERLESSNESS VS CHOICE

Negative	Positive
Believing you have no choice	Recognising that there is choice
Blaming other people	Taking responsibility
Feeling powerless	Learning to take healthy control
Abstaining from decision making	Making decisions
Waiting for recovery to happen	Being proactive in working towards recovery

When driven by the need to self-harm, it can feel as if you are powerless to change; that you don't have the ability to choose. An important part of our functioning, the volitional aspect, concerns will and choice: in everything we do, we have a choice that ultimately will either help or hinder recovery.

In the book of Deuteronomy in the Old Testament, God says to the Israelites, 'This day I call heaven and earth as witnesses against you that I have set before you life and death, blessings and curses. Now choose life, so that you and your children may live' (Deut. 30:19); our choices affect us physically, emotionally and spiritually. For me (Abbie) this scripture was the turning point of my recovery as I saw it in black and white terms – life or death – which jolted me into taking action. Let's look at what this means:

Choice A (Death) = choices that hurt me, pull me away from God and keep me in the past.

Choice B (Life) = choices that heal me, draw me closer to God and help me to grow.

When faced with different options or pulled to carry out a particular action, we need to ask ourselves, 'Does it fall into Choice A or B?' The first will pull you back into the self-harm cycle; the second will spur you on towards recovery.

Perhaps you are drawn to Choice A because it's all you have known and hurting yourself actually gives you a sense of power; you fear that in letting go you will be even more powerless. One of the greatest gifts you can give yourself is to learn that life does not have to control you: instead you can make choices, choices that empower you.

PAUSE FOR THOUGHT

In your recovery book you might like to write down negative choices you have made (Choice A) and what positive choices you could make next time (Choice B). We've given some examples below:

Choice A (Death)	Choice B (Life)
Couldn't cope so I had to cut.	Talk to someone about how I feel.
Believed what my head said, 'You will never get better' and felt really low.	Fight what my head says, read testimonies of people who have recovered.
Made sure I had my self-harm implements easy to hand, even under my pillow, so I could access them the minute I felt bad.	Choose to keep self-harm tools away from easy access and put a note on top saying, 'You don't have to do this, there are alternatives.'

The more you practice making healthy choices, the easier it becomes. It feels really good when you make a positive choice and manage to follow through on it – you break the powerlessness inside which keeps you captive.

RATIONAL: MISBELIEF VS TRUTH

Negative	Positive
Telling yourself you can't change the way you think	Learning to challenge your thinking
Believing you can't help the way you feel	Correcting thoughts to change your feelings
Thoughts being controlled by past hurts	Thoughts being grounded in the present
Telling yourself that you are bad, horrid, useless, etc	Speaking positives about yourself

Our minds are very powerful. The Bible says: 'Be careful how you think; your life is shaped by your thoughts' (Proverbs 4:23 GNB). How you think affects the way you feel and the choices you make.

Albert Ellis, a clinical psychologist, developed what he terms The ABC Theory of Emotion[1]

A = the activating event

B = the belief system

C = the consequent emotion

D = destructive behaviour (added by the authors)

Albert Ellis' point is that it is not the event in itself that results in the emotion, but rather what you *believe* or *say* about the event. For instance if someone you know walks straight past you, you can feel hurt. Why? Because you may be saying to yourself, 'I'm not important' or 'She purposely didn't say hello'. If, instead, your response is, 'She's obviously in a hurry or didn't see me' then you do not feel so hurt and rejected.

What's playing in your head?
Our heads are like a huge CD library full of tracks of things we say to ourselves based on life experiences. Negative words, which are not entirely true and are influenced by the past, are known as misbeliefs, such as:

'I'm never going to be perfect so there's no point trying.'

'If I cry it shows I'm weak.'

'I deserve to be punished.'

'I can never recover because of what was done to me.'

'Hurting myself is the only way of coping with life.'

'Other people are better than I am.'

'Other people's opinions count, mine don't.'

What else might you add?

We all play unhelpful tracks over and over again in our heads. The key is learning to recognise them and practise changing them for more helpful thought patterns.

Where do the tracks come from?

The wrong messages we play to ourselves normally come from what we saw, heard or felt in childhood or at another time when we were particularly vulnerable. People who have any kind of power or authority over us will implant ideas that we treat as fact until we challenge them. These could be parents or other primary caregivers; grandparents, or other extended family members; babysitters or child-minders; teachers; priests, pastors and youth leaders; friends, peers or bullies, or TV personalities.

Can you think of negative words that were said to you, about you or inferred? Negative messages have as much sticking power as positive ones but in the stages of forming personality we can't differentiate between them. Until we learn how to challenge what we say to ourselves, we act as though those negative words are fact.

Many of the tracks we play tend to be either exaggerated or black and white, such as:

'People being angry or criticising me is intolerable.'

'It's disastrous when things go wrong.'

'If I don't self-harm straight away it's the end of the world.'

'Self-harm makes me a bad person.'

'If the cut isn't deep enough it won't work.'

'If I don't self-harm I'll never survive.'

The following words are often used when thinking in this way – if you catch yourself using them, bear in mind that they usually lead to a negative spiral.

Always
Impossible
Ruined
Never
Awful
Disastrous
Perfect
Terrible
Furious

Try finding less drastic, more open words such as:
'Sometimes' instead of 'Always'
'Not great' instead of 'Disastrous'
'Somewhat spoilt' instead of 'Ruined'
'Pretty difficult' instead of 'Impossible'

Correcting thinking

As thoughts arise, or as you recognise what thoughts lie behind your negative feelings, you need to challenge your distorted thinking and replace it with reality/truth.

Thought: 'I should never upset other people.'

Challenge: 'Am I responsible for other people's feelings?'

Truth: 'I can't avoid accidentally upsetting others sometimes and I am not responsible for their feelings or reactions.'

Thought: 'If people really cared they would know what I need.'

Challenge: 'Is it fair to expect other people to guess what I need?'

Truth: 'Just because a person doesn't guess what I need it doesn't mean they don't care. It's unreasonable to expect them to guess, and it's up to me to ask for what I need.'

SPIRITUAL: SELF-REJECTION VS SELF-WORTH

Negative	Positive
Always speaking negatives about yourself	Getting to know your strengths and weaknesses
Self-rejection, hatred, loathing	Self-worth and affirmation
Seeking to find your identity and worth in people, possessions, achievement, etc	Knowing your identity and worth as a child of God, receiving His unconditional love
Looking to other people to validate you	Validating yourself

At the core of most addictive, self-destructive patterns are strong negative attitudes towards yourself. With which of the following phrases can you identity?

'I hate/loathe myself.'

'I don't know who I am.'

'I'm not special.'

'I'm a nobody.'

'I'm not as good as other people.'

'I should never have been born.'

'I'm not like others.'

'I don't deserve to be accepted.'

'I'm worthless.'

'I wish I was dead.'

'I don't belong.'

'I'm revolting.'

The core shame and loathing at the root of many addictive patterns needs to change in order to bring about lasting freedom. If it doesn't, then the danger is that the addictive pattern may re-emerge in another form, hence someone who self-harms turns to an eating disorder or exercise addiction and vice versa. The question is: how can you go from self-rejection, hatred and little sense of identity, to self-acceptance, worth and feelings of belonging and being of value?

To make such a shift it's necessary to look at the foundation upon which you have built your beliefs about yourself. Are they based on what other people have said, experiences you have had and your own wavering emotions, or what the Bible teaches about you being made in the image of God?

The trouble with basing our worth on what other people say or on what we do, achieve, or earn is that all these can shift too easily. Our true value needs to be based on the unchangeable: Hebrews 13:8 says that God is the same yesterday, today and forever. I don't want to feel valuable one minute and not the next, do you? Our identity and value is in our origin: as children of God. We are made in the image of God and He paid the price for our wrongdoing through Jesus, the perfect sacrifice – fully human and fully God – dying in our place in order that we can know what it is to be forgiven and to live in His presence forever.

Nothing will cause God to love you less and nothing will make Him love you more. To accept ourselves we need first to know what it is to be truly loved: God is the only source of unconditional love.

We first need to know God for who He really is:

unfailing love Psalm 36:7
faithful to His promises Psalm 145:13
truly good Luke 18:19
compassionate Isaiah 30:18
slow to anger Numbers 14:18
full of wisdom Psalm 36:6 (TLB)

forgiving 1 John 1:9
rich in mercy Ephesians 2:4–5
able to do anything Job 42:2
unchanging James 1:17
full of grace and truth John 1:14
full of tender kindness Psalm 89:1 (TLB)
perfect in His understanding Job 36:5 (TLB)
just Deuteronomy 32:4

Then we need to realise who we are as His children:
precious and honoured Isaiah 43:4
loved 1 John 4:10
heirs to a throne Galatians 4:7
accepted Romans 15:7
forgiven Colossians 3:13

Tips for an improved self-worth

In addition to discovering your incredible value, there are other small steps you can take to improve your sense of worth. Stop comparing yourself to other people: you are unique. Let go of perfection and aim for 'good enough'. Set realistic expectations for yourself and others. Don't put yourself down: when you do so, you are saying God didn't do a good enough job when He made you. Get into the habit of thinking and saying positive things about yourself and to yourself. Accept compliments: you need to be nurtured to heal. Use self-help books and websites to help you change your beliefs. Spend time with positive and supportive people. Acknowledge your positive qualities and things you are good at. Be assertive and don't allow people to treat you with a lack of respect. Engage in work and hobbies that you enjoy.

REFLECTION

There is always a choice between doing that which harms us and doing that which heals. To make choices that heal we need to turn to the one true Healer, who heals the brokenhearted and binds up their wounds – read Psalm 147.

ACTION

You may like to draw a table with all the negative thoughts that keep occurring on one side and ways in which you could correct them on the other. Why not ask someone you know who is good at challenging thinking to come up with some realistic but positive sentences to replace the negative ones.

PRAYER

Dear God, please help me to see that I have choices in life – both in what I choose to do or think, and in what I believe about how You feel about me. Jesus, help me to see that I am worth everything to You, and to treat myself as such. Amen.

CHAPTER 9

TIMES OF RELAPSE

THE UPS AND DOWNS

After you have set your heart on no longer self-harming, you can be flooded with feelings of disappointment and hopelessness when you find yourself reaching for your old coping mechanism. Perhaps you see recovery as a long gradual uphill climb and so view any dips as negative. In reality, recovery is very up and down!

When I (Abbie) was helping on a residential course, one of the girls mentioned how every time she made progress in her recovery and reached new heights (like climbing a mountain) she would slip and fall back down (into the valley). She felt frustrated and negative, and believed she would never recover. As I prayed I had a picture. It was of a trampoline in the valley. I felt God say that whilst she may at this stage trip and fall down the mountainside she would learn from her experiences, land on the trampoline and be propelled up again. God also showed me that each valley she came across was less deep than the previous one. She is now fully recovered and supporting others on their journeys to freedom.

Coming to terms with the fact that recovery is not linear but up and down (whilst still moving forward) is important because it helps you to be more realistic about expectations and kinder to yourself, and encourages you to stay motivated to get better.

Linear   **Up and Down**

In my own journey I (Abbie) remember at times thinking that I was a failure because in comparison to other people's stories (even Helena's) it appeared that their recovery had been simple: it was as though they listened to God and those helping, put spiritual and therapeutic principles into operation and moved on. I, on the other hand, was constantly getting stuck, battling with principles and feeling like little progress was made. It was frustrating and demoralising. I had to realise that no one's journey is necessarily easy and that there are key lessons to be learned that create endurance, character, and internal strength.

A few reminders
- A slip up does not mean that you have returned to square one, because along the journey you will have learnt some lessons, gained insights and picked up a few tools.

- Turning to self-harm when you have not done so for a while does not make you a failure, nor does it mean you will continue down this route forever.
- Having lost some ground does not mean you can't regain it. Be careful not to use it as an excuse to keep going down the slippery slope.
- Other people may be frustrated with you and say unhelpful words, but you do not have to take these on board. You have fallen over and can pick yourself up again.
- If you managed to go without self-harming for a period you can do it again. Remind yourself of what it was that helped last time.
- There's a reason you have slipped back into self-harming. Try to be objective. Look at what changes have taken place in your life recently or what else needs to change.
- Consider whether you have stopped using any of the tools that helped previously. Are you still keeping up with writing in your recovery book, or another notebook? Are you continuing to talk openly with someone who understands? Do you have outlets to express your feelings and are you correcting misbeliefs?
- Do you need to have some counselling or therapy, talk to the pastoral team at church or make contact with a self-harm forum? It is not a sign of weakness to go back to having extra help.

WHAT STOPS CHANGE?

We (the authors) believe that the reason people find it hard to change is because there is something missing, not because they are one of the few who can't recover. Change can be complex and messy. Knoster, Villa & Thousand[1] have researched and written much on the dynamics of change. They highlight that for change to occur, various factors need to be in place (see the top line of the chart below). If one of the elements is missing it results in a particular reaction (the words in italic).

Vision	Skills	Incentives	Resources	Action plan	=	Change
	Skills	Incentives	Resources	Action plan	=	*Confusion*
Vision		Incentives	Resources	Action plan	=	*Anxiety*
Vision	Skills		Resources	Action plan	=	*Resistance*
Vision	Skills	Incentives		Action plan	=	*Frustration*
Vision	Skills	Incentives	Resources		=	*Treadmill*

To summarise:
without vision, you end up *confused*
without skills, you end up *anxious*
without incentives, you end up *resistant*
without resources, you end up *frustrated*
without an action plan, you end up on a *treadmill*

Vision
Vision is the big picture of what you want to accomplish. A vision for recovery needs to be more than just 'I want to get better.' It might be 'I want to stop self-harming, finish my teacher training and work abroad' or 'I want to stop self-harming so I can go back to my job as a children's nurse.' You need to create a vision for your life and then work backwards: what do you need to accomplish in order to fulfill the vision? Once a vision is established, it is necessary to build the skills needed to realise the vision. If you lack a sense of vision it can leave you feeling confused; if you don't know where you are going you won't know

what steps to take to get there.

Someone once said: 'A man without a vision is a man without a future. A man without a future will always return to his past.' Proverbs 29:18 says, 'Where there is no vision, the people are unrestrained, But happy is he who keeps the law' (NASB).

In order to help you explore 'Vision' ask yourself questions like:

'Do I have goals and things to look forward to – a reason to get better?'

'What could I do when recovered that I can't do now?'

'Do I have dreams, hopes and aspirations for the future?'

'What do I want to achieve and why?'

'Do I have direction and a sense of where I am going?'

'How would I like things to be different?'

'Where would I like life to be in five years time – can this be a magnet to pull me forward?'

Skills
If you are feeling anxious it is quite likely that you lack some of the skills needed to maintain recovery. Some of the skills you could work on are:

Asking for help, if needed.

Saying 'no' when you mean 'no' and setting boundaries.

Delaying self-harm to look at what is happening.

Learning to identify and express emotions.

Making sure life has a balance of work, play and rest.

Developing assertiveness, communication and confidence.[2]

Looking at not being a victim, persecutor or rescuer.[2]

Learning to understand the difference between safe and unsafe people.[2]

Incentives

If you are feeling resistant to change then it suggests that incentives are missing. They are the reasons for getting better. You will discover your incentives by answering the question, 'Why do I want to stop self-harming?' These are some answers that people have given:

'I want to travel and don't want to be self-harming.'

'I don't want my children to be affected any more than they have been.'

'I am getting married and don't want it to affect my marriage.'

'I want to wear short sleeves in the summer.'

'I don't want any more scars.'

'I want to honour my body as I have begun to realise that it is the temple of the Holy Spirit.'

Resources

A feeling of frustration suggests that you want to recover, but don't seem to have the necessary resources in place. Resources include:

Websites and literature (including this book)

Professional help (GP, CPN and counsellor)

Friends and those you know who can offer support and accountability

An emergency contact list (see Chapter 6)

Teaching days, courses (see useful resources at the end of the book)

Stories of recovery (books, DVDs, blogs and YouTube)

Action Plan

If you are feeling as if you are going round and round in circles in your recovery, a plan of action may be lacking. In Chapter 6 we considered plans and focused on SMART goals. Spend a little time revisiting what was said and draw up the way forward for your recovery. Show it to someone you trust and together, if appropriate, pray that God will give you what you need to overcome self-harm.

PAUSE FOR THOUGHT

When you look at your journey in light of the above, do you think there are areas missing? Think about how you might instigate vision, skills, incentives, resources or an action plan, and write it in your recovery book.

SELF-ASSESSMENT – HALT!

To prevent and deal with relapse you need to become more familiar with assessing your own reactions to people and situations, or changes in circumstance that potentially act as triggers. One technique you can use is HALT which has its origins in addiction recovery programmes. It is a simple yet incredibly useful method for identifying what may lie behind the urge to self-harm or carry out any other unhealthy behaviour or coping mechanism. Ask yourself: 'Am I feeling any of the following?'

Hungry
Angry
Lonely
Tired

Hungry

Hunger can make you feel really low and irrational. It is important to keep a healthy blood sugar level by eating regularly and having a snack if hungry. What you eat when needing a snack is important. Some foods cause a sudden rise followed by a sudden dip in blood sugar such as cakes and biscuits, so it's best to avoid these. You are better eating wholemeal bread, nuts and seeds or crackers and cheese.

Angry

Anger is an emotion with which many self-harmers struggle, whether the difficulty is in controlling it or recognising it. Remember, it's OK to feel angry. You don't have to self-harm in response to it. There are other options. Sometimes allowing yourself to sit with anger and work out if it's justified is all you need to make it feel easier. Bear the following in mind:

- Behind anger there is often a *blocked goal*. Ask yourself what you want to achieve that is being blocked in some way.
- All emotions are like waves: they reach a peak and come down again. Your feelings won't go on forever and you don't have to bring them to an end by hurting yourself.
- You can express anger through talking and writing or through an action-based activity: sports, a fast console game.
- You can reduce the intensity of anger by thinking of something sad and also by challenging your negative thoughts and self-talk (see Chapter 8).

Lonely

Feeling lonely can happen when alone or with people. In addition to circumstances, it is also about our relationship with ourselves. There are different types of loneliness.[3] It is important to identify why you are lonely: is it because you are spending time on your own, you are not connecting closely with others or you feel misunderstood?

The middle of the night can be the loneliest time for some

people, and it's difficult to do anything about it. When I (Abbie) used to feel lonely in the night I would write letters. Although I wasn't physically with people I was communicating with them, which made me feel less alone. Prayer was also a real comfort to me – God doesn't sleep at night: He's always there, waiting to listen.

If you are lonely during the day, try to break it down into manageable time slots and consider what you are going to do with each period, such as: 'I will go for a walk for half an hour and when I get back I will put the washing on, make a coffee and see if a friend is in for a chat. If no one is free to meet up this afternoon I will read a book, write my thoughts and feelings down and then pick a programme to watch on TV.'

If you feel especially low and at risk, don't forget that there are helplines such as The Samaritans (08457 90 90 90) and ChildLine (0800 11 11).

Tired

Tiredness can be responsible for rash decisions, moments of weakness, giving in and not having the energy to fight unhelpful urges. Getting sufficient sleep is vital. If you don't sleep well try taking power naps. I (Helena) work long hours but I do listen to my body when it indicates I need rest. On these occasions I lie down and rest or sleep for ten minutes or even an hour (time permitting) and then feel able to get going again. Sometimes work or lifestyle don't allow for this – I (Abbie) have small children who don't like it when I disappear for a nap, so I have to be very strict with myself about getting at least eight hours of sleep at night.

Aim to take regular exercise – the release of endorphins will give you a greater sense of well-being and help you sleep (so long as it's not done just before bed). If you find that you are constantly tired, you may need to make changes to your routine or ensure you don't have coffee or sugar in the evenings. If you carry on being tired, visit your GP for a checkup.

Don't give up!
However smooth or bumpy your journey to recovery, it's important not to give up hope. Keep putting into practice all you are learning through reading this book (and other forms of help). Believe that you *will* reach the place of no longer needing to self-harm; in time it will become a pattern of the past.

REFLECTION
Recovery will always involve ups and downs – as does life after recovery. Learning how to deal with these ups and downs is what enables us to live the full life that God has planned for us.

ACTION
Everyone gets hungry, angry, lonely or tired. In your recovery book, write down ways you can deal with each of these so that when the situation arises you are already prepared.

PRAYER
Dear God, sometimes the journey to freedom seems too tough. I feel like I'm not getting anywhere and even going backwards at times. Lord Jesus, please help me to stay focused and place my hope in You. Amen.

CHAPTER 10

HELPING SUFFERERS (PERSONAL)

WHAT DO I DO?

When you know that someone you care about is self-harming your mind is inevitably filled with lots of thoughts and questions:

'Do I raise the subject?'

'Is it OK to talk about it?'

'Why is the person self-harming?'

'Have I done anything to contribute?'

'Is it helpful or unhelpful to ask to see wounds?'

'What can I do to help?'

'I'm unsure what to do in case I make it worse.'

'When I try to approach the subject I get rebuffed, so what's the point.'

'I have to protect the person, not let this happen.'

'I need to understand.'

'How come I didn't notice before?'

'Why has she/he kept it a secret?'

With all these thoughts going on it can be hard to know how to react, but try to be yourself, stay calm, listen and don't judge, punish or panic.

In order to open up, people need to feel safe and not fear that their way of coping will be ripped away from them, misinterpreted and misunderstood. Even if the initial reaction from the self-harmer is negative, showing care towards someone is never wasted. They will retain the memory and will talk in time. What's important is setting the right scene for supporting them.

When you first discover that the person is self-harming it's easy to dig for answers, blame yourself, be impatient, go down the 'if only' route or make assumptions about why they are doing it. Jerusha Clark says, 'You can best honor those you love by observing the signs, praying diligently, opening the door for others to share their struggles, and confronting behaviours when needed.'[1]

You will naturally want to stop the person self-harming; some parents and partners talk about hiding the kitchen knives, locking away matches and lighters, or sneaking into bedrooms to search for implements. Contrary to how you feel, it's best to avoid these measures initially. Self-harm is a method of communication and self-management of emotion, therefore the danger is that since the underlying issues still exist the person will turn to an unfamiliar way of harming themselves. This can cause more harm.

TIPS FOR TALKING TO THE SELF-HARMER

Prepare what to say: Take some time to plan how you are going to initiate a conversation with the person. Jot your thoughts down and bounce your ideas off a trusted friend.

Choose your place and time: The right location and time can assist a person to open up. It's best not to raise the topic of self-harm when you are in a busy place where people can overhear and children can interrupt.

Make sure you give the person undivided attention: If you are clock-watching, answering texts or looking out for someone to arrive, you will unintentionally give the message that what the person is sharing isn't important. Avoid talking when you are tired or raising the subject when already in a tense situation or restricted on time.

The person may find it easier if they are occupied such as going for a walk, baking, stroking an animal or engaging in a hobby. This helps to avoid constant eye contact, which can make a person feel vulnerable and exposed.

Be prepared for negative reactions: The first response to support may be negative because the person may not be ready to talk, or feel vulnerable, ashamed or fearful of your response. If they refuse to talk don't take it personally, simply offer them the opportunity to do so when they are ready.

Be aware of your limits: People who self-harm often feel overwhelmed by emotional pain and pre-occupied with self-destructive thoughts. This can result in a sense of urgency for support, so being clear about what you can consistently offer is crucial. This is both for your own physical and emotional health and the long-term well-being of the person who is self-harming.

AS A PARENT OF A SELF-HARMER

When you find out that your own child is self-harming it can hit hard. As a family member there can be the thought of, 'this isn't happening in our family'; to the sufferer there can be times when it feels like the person who self-harms is actually 'another you'.

> Janet says
>
> 'I'm the mother of a beautiful 13-year-old girl. As a young child she used to curl up with her head on my knee, tell me she loved me and fall asleep. Her affectionate, gentle, artistic, sensitive nature made me the proudest mum. Never in a million years did it occur to me that Lily would do anything to hurt herself. I was shell-shocked when the school rang one afternoon to say that Lily had self-harmed, needed to go to A&E and it wasn't the first time she'd cut herself. My head felt in a whirl: disbelief, fear, grief and anger all fought for space. It was as if the head teacher was speaking about someone else's child. Surely there was a mistake? I was thrown into a world of chaos, confusion and powerlessness.'

The NSPCC offer the following advice for parents:[2]

Provide first aid: Paying attention to the injuries can show your child that their body is worth caring about. Don't just focus on the injuries, as it's important to understand how difficult the young person is finding life.

Let your child know you care about them: You may not be a person they can talk to at the moment, but let them know you want to help. Praise the small things they do. If their self-esteem is low they will need all the encouragement you can give them.

Listen if they want to talk: If they do start talking, just listen. You can show you are listening by summarising what they have told you in your own words. This may help them to think more clearly when they hear their story repeated back to them. It is important not to try to problem-solve or manage their situation. Ask them what they want you to do. Sometimes it can be difficult to talk face to face with a parent. Carla, whose daughter Lizzie self-harms, often has text, Facetime and Skype conversations with her daughter, even though they are only in next-door bedrooms. This reduces the stress for both of them, but keeps avenues of communication open.

Encourage them to get help: Provide the first-aid they need for cuts but insist they get medical attention for anything that looks serious. Tell them that this is not normal or healthy behaviour but there are people who can help them find better ways to cope.

Stay calm but be persistent: It is important you don't get upset or angry. Persist in your request for them to get help. Use the cracked record approach and reiterate that: 'I can see you are really upset, but you need to talk to someone who knows more about this than me. You need to get help.'

Get support for yourself: Dealing with your child's emotions, your own reaction, and managing other members of the family and their needs can be completely overwhelming. Talk to your family doctor, find a friend you trust or look for support groups locally or online. You cannot help your child if you become ill yourself.

You can also call the NSPCC helpline at any time of day or night on 0808 800 5000 or download a free booklet, 'Listening to Children' for some useful advice.

In addition to parents, other family members will need the space to talk about their own feelings. Disclosing to another family member is best done with the permission and knowledge of the self-harmer, appropriate to the age of the person. It can be very difficult for siblings to understand about self-harm but, depending on their age, they can play a significant role in coming alongside the sufferer, so long as this does not impose a burden and the sibling's needs are responded to equally. If the siblings are young it may not be necessary to explain in detail but rather to say something along the following lines, 'Sarah is very sad and we are trying to help make her happy again,' letting the child ask their own questions. For older siblings, the tips for friends may be useful.

AS A FRIEND/PARTNER OF A SELF-HARMER

Finding out that your friend or partner self-harms can be challenging and stir up emotions. Remember that whatever they disclose, even if it is upsetting, does not have to threaten the friendship or relationship. They are still the same person despite changes in behaviour.

Tips for helping

- Let them know that you care and you will stick by them, but don't be frightened to say that you are a bit apprehensive about self-harm (if you are).
- Encourage them to talk but don't push and remember that listening is more important than speaking.
- Remember your main role is as a *friend* not a carer or therapist. Don't try to solve the self-harm, to parent or to sort the person out.
- It may be helpful to suggest that they speak to someone who can help. Assist them to consider who would be the most appropriate person.

- If they need moral support when speaking to someone you could offer to go with them but encourage *them* to be the one to do the talking.
- Try not to let the self-harm rob you of the friendship or relationship or stop you enjoying each other's company.
- Read about self-harm, as insight can bring reassurance and help you to know how to respond.
- Don't make assumptions that they self-harm for a particular reason; let them explain.
- Don't talk to others about the person. They need to be the one to inform people when the time is right.
- Even though it is not helpful to talk to others (gossip) about them, you will need a safe person to whom you can offload. It's a big burden to carry alone.
- If they endeavour to swear you to secrecy, reassure them you will keep confidences and will not divulge information unnecessarily, but for their own safety you may need to talk about what has happened and also about your feelings.
- Be aware of what you can and can't do. You can't fix everything. There will almost always need to be other people involved.
- Be aware of your role and the roles of others.
- It's best not to ask to see the injuries unless you are really concerned that the person needs medical help.
- Remember that self-harm is your friend's way of expressing pain or stress and she or he will need to learn healthy ways of expression and coping; it can't just stop immediately.
- Bear in mind that there may need to be a period when the person is both self-harming and learning new coping strategies.
- Try not to exclude the person from any social plans or groups because you think they won't want to socialise – give them the

choice of whether to join in.

- Remember you are in a unique position to foster healthy lifestyle choices outside the issue of self-harm without being judgmental or patronising.
- Take care of yourself. You have needs too. It can be hard work supporting someone so make sure you don't take on their problems.

Natalya is a close friend of someone who self-harms. This is her advice:

'Don't be afraid to ask if they have self-harmed or if they have wanted to. Be practical and understanding, but don't get too sympathetic – you need to show that although you can understand the self-harm, you still want it to stop. Don't take the emotions of your friend on board; you can't stop them self-harming. Do fun things with your friend too, don't let every meeting or conversation be all about self-harm. And if you know each other really well, allow yourself to have a sense of humour about it – laughter can ease tension when talking about even the most difficult things.'

Natalya also makes the point that it is important to support but not become overwhelmed by the issue of self-harm: to love and let go.

'I talk to my friend, listen and support her. Then I go home, talk to God, take all my concerns to Him, and leave them there. I don't have to keep worrying about her. My friend isn't a burden for me because I leave that burden with God.'

REFLECTION

Time is important. Just because someone isn't ready to talk now, it doesn't mean she or he never will be. And remember, blame never helps – whether it's blaming yourself or the self-harmer you care about.

ACTION

If you are a carer, use the 'tips for helping' to consider the best ways to talk to the person you are supporting and write your thoughts down. If you a self-harmer, which of the tips would you find most helpful? Write these down so that you can share them with the person or people supporting you.

PRAYER

Dear God, You know how much I want _____ to be free from self-harm and what they most need in order to recover. Please help me to be sensitive to their needs and do what is best, even if it is different from how I would normally operate. Amen.

CHAPTER 11

HELPING SUFFERERS (THERAPEUTIC)

ATTITUDES AND ACTIONS

The person who self-harms is often treated differently from those with other issues because the problem is self-inflicted. Their appearance or manner may reinforce this further. In many cases they are seen as less of a priority, as the following account reveals.

I (Helena) was running a residential course during which one of the delegates self-harmed. A colleague and I took her to A&E where we found ourselves witnessing people being seen who had arrived several hours after us. At one point we were the only ones in A&E. Eight hours later a doctor saw the girl. 'We've had some *very sick* people in tonight,' she said. No doubt this was true but her tone of voice suggested that emotionally sick people who have physical wounds are somehow less deserving of treatment than those who are physically sick.

Sadly, many people who self-harm recount unhelpful

interactions with the medical profession; a few speak highly of their experiences. Of course bad experiences are, in part, due to the self-harmer's reactive responses, fear and inner pain, but by no means entirely. Whatever your role in helping a sufferer, be it emergency services, crisis team, GP or therapist, compassion, understanding and insight are crucial as they pave the way for further help. One of the greatest concerns that many self-harmers have is that they will be seen as time wasters and be misunderstood. Reassuring them that their needs are just as valid as anyone else's will make a big difference.

It is important to set aside personal feelings and prejudices and to see beyond the behaviour of the person who carries pain, confusion, memories and insecurities and to ensure that the care given does not rob the person of autonomy and dignity. To aid this process it is useful to look at the style of communication you use with sufferers. Below are unhelpful comments and actions reported by self-harmers and suggested helpful responses.

UNHELPFUL COMMENTS:

'Honestly, what did you do that for?'
'You'll have scars forever.'
'You'll grow out of it.'
'What a crazy thing to do.'
'Why would you try to kill yourself?'
'I've seen worse.'
'It's attention seeking.'
'Pull yourself together.'
'Think of the people you're hurting.'
'You're wasting our time – we have really sick people here.'

UNHELPFUL ACTIONS:

- ignoring injuries because they are self inflicted
- ignoring the self-harmer and only concentrating on injuries
- treating wounds without a local anaesthetic to teach them a lesson
- using drug-only treatment without counselling or therapy
- treating them as irresponsible or disturbed
- making assumptions
- sighing, not making eye contact or using other body language to give a message of disapproval
- speaking to the person accompanying the self-harmer instead of the self-harmer
- taking self-harm away without looking at replacement coping strategies (inpatient setting)

HELPFUL RESPONSES:

It is important to have a non-judgmental attitude as the following questions indicate. This allows the person to talk about their self-harm without shame and with the freedom to express their feelings, if they can.

'How are you?' – the simple questions are often the best.

'You must have been feeling really bad' – acknowledging emotional pain, not just physical.

'Tell me if I hurt you' – recognising that injuries are just as painful when self-inflicted.

'Are you managing to look after your wounds?' – helping them to consider the practicalities.

'Are you able to say why you self-harmed?' – giving the chance to explain without pushing.

'Has anyone helped you look at alternatives to self-harm?' –

providing some suggestions.

'Would you feel less alone if you joined a support group or online forum?'

'What would help now?' – encouraging the person to make choices rather than dictating what's going to be done.

If they want to talk, ask questions such as the following but reassure them that they are not under pressure to answer:

'What happened just before you felt the need to harm yourself?'

'What were you feeling?'

'How does self-harm help?'

'Do you want to stop … do you need help to stop?'

'Can you explain what happens?'

'Is there anything it would be helpful to share?'

'What can I do to help?'

PAUSE FOR THOUGHT

When working with self-harmers in a medical setting, have you ever found yourself dealing with them in a way that doesn't acknowledge the emotional pain behind the physical wounds? How could you change your reactions in future?

THERAPEUTIC HELP

Counsellors and therapists will generally work more intensely and closely with sufferers than anyone else. Below are considerations specifically relevant when working with a client.

CONSIDERATIONS

Prior to counselling or therapy, decide on your ground rules regarding self-harming behaviour. In addition to a counselling contract do you use self-harm contracts? Below are different approaches:

No harm: this is where therapy is ended or suspended if a client self-harms. Many sufferers find this very damaging if they don't have sufficient support whilst the no-harm contract is in place. This type of contract may involve the client being able to contact the therapist between sessions if the urge to self-harm occurs. If, however, self-harm is still carried out, there is a time period before therapy can be undertaken again, allowing the client to examine for themselves why they self-harmed.

No harm in sessions: this keeps the therapy as a safe place and is respectful of both therapist and self-harmer. Either there are no restrictions on self-harming outside of sessions, or this could be used in conjunction with the two contracts below.

Contact before self-harm: this requires the self-harmer to make contact with someone on their safe list before self-harming, empowering the client to make choices, bringing what the client may feel as shameful thoughts and behaviour into the open.

Seek to identify what role this powerful coping mechanism plays in your client's life, as it is the key to understanding what is going on and what is needed to effect change. Examine your own motives for wanting your client to cease or stabilise their self-harming as soon as possible. If it is because you are not comfortable this can create a power struggle or force the client into secretly self-harming, resulting in distrust and reducing the effectiveness of the therapeutic alliance. Help the client think through a safe way for dealing with crisis situations. This could include whom the client would contact, where to go for medical help and what support may be needed, and how to use grounding skills (see Chapter 4, 'Tips for dealing with triggers').

Since successful treatment of self-harm depends heavily on trust and on teaching the client new ways of coping, hospitalisation is best used only as a last resort if the client is at risk of suicide or severe self-harm. Talk with your client about the procedure should this be necessary.

USEFUL TECHNIQUES

There are a number of useful techniques and exercises that you can use with clients who self-harm. The book *The Decider: A Skills Manual* by Michelle Ayres and Carol Vivyan has lots of ideas and the pages can be copied and given to clients to use. We've made some suggestions below, but this is by no means an exhaustive list.

SCALING

Scaling questions have developed into the most well-known and frequently used solution-focused techniques and are proving very beneficial with people who self-harm. Scaling involves asking the client to grade how they feel on a scale of one to ten, and then explore ways in which this can be changed by simple actions – for example, reducing a score of 8 for emotional pain, which *would* include self-harm, to a 6, that *wouldn't* include self-harm, by writing down feelings and then tearing up the paper.

Using scaling in therapy helps clients to break down their perception of the situation into grades by asking questions that precipitate change. It assists them in putting limits around the experience so that it no longer feels uncontrollable or endless and becomes more manageable and hopeful. It also helps them to step outside their experience by observing it and engaging the non-emotional part of the brain to scale their experience of pain, anxiety or fear. Using this method gets the self-harmer over the urge to self-harm very effectively, and builds confidence in their own ability to resist self-harming outside therapy.

JOURNALING

Encouraging self-harmers to write in the form of a journal can be very useful – many of them already will. Journaling is a great tool to encourage in therapy as it gives you the counsellor insight into the client's behaviour between sessions.

EXERCISES

Research seems to suggest that self-harmers have a more time-limited view than other clients, meaning that their attention span is shorter. This is why paper-based exercises are useful, because, like self-harm, they offer immediate answers or gratification of some sort. Anything concrete is good to use in working with self-harmers; it doesn't have to be directly related to self-harm. We (the authors) have both used tools to assist in recognising emotions, acknowledging unhelpful thought patterns, setting boundaries and devising a recovery plan.

For some helpful examples of written exercises, read *Bodily Harm*, by Karen Conterio and Wendy Lader, published by Hyperion.

IMPULSE CONTROL LOG

At the SAFE (Self Abuse Finally Ends) Alternatives Clinic in America, therapists use what is called an Impulse Control Log to help sufferers slow down their behaviour. It recognises that the wish to self-harm stems from a thought, not a feeling, and that thoughts can be consciously changed. Every time a patient feels the urge to self-harm, they make entries in a journal under each of nine headings:

Self-harm thoughts
Time and date
Location
Situation
Feeling
What would be the result of self-harm?
What would I be trying to communicate?
Action taken
Outcome

This can be a useful tool for the self-harmer to avoid harming when outside of therapy sessions, and valuable for the therapist to see what the process is behind the client's self-harming. For more details on impulse control logs, again the book *Bodily Harm* is useful.

CREATIVE THERAPY

All sorts of things can be used to encourage clients to open up – the only limit is your imagination! Between us (the authors) we have used stones, buttons, teddies, blankets, pets, Play-Doh®, drawing, and much more. Play therapy is not just for children – it can work really well with adults and adolescents who are finding it hard to express themselves. For example, instead of asking a client to explain how he or she feels, ask them to draw how they feel. Ask them to model their pain in Play-Doh®, or ask them which cuddly toy they most relate to and why. Having tactile things in a counselling room can be very valuable for an agitated client – just having a stress ball to fiddle with or a colouring book to colour can help with talking.

REFLECTION

Every self-harmer is different, so there is no one-size-fits-all approach to therapy. Treating each client as an individual and listening to what each sufferer finds helpful is the only path towards freedom from self-harm.

ACTION

If you are a self-harmer, which of the above methods appeal to you? Write ideas in your notebook to take to counselling. If you are a professional, consider which of the approaches above would be useful with your clients and put some into action.

PRAYER

Dear God, thank You for giving me the opportunity to work with self-harmers. I pray that You give me wisdom and direct me each step of the way. Amen.

CHAPTER 12

HELPING SUFFERERS (CHURCH)

BEING APPROACHABLE

People have the tendency to shy away from speaking with self-harmers once they have found out that's what they do. What do you say? What if you put your foot in it? One of the most important contributions anyone can make is to just *be yourself*. Too often in churches there is a hidden message that you have to keep a smile on your face when your world is falling apart. People who self-harm need to know that the person with whom they are engaging is genuine and that they can be too. Try not to treat the person differently but at the same time be mindful that certain actions can either hinder or help. If you think, 'Oh, no, I've said or done the wrong thing,' acknowledge it and apologise – no one gets it right all the time.

LEADERS

As a leader or member of a leadership team, do you portray a willingness to come alongside people from all walks of life including someone who uses challenging coping mechanisms, appears secretive, is needy one minute and pushes people away the next? The response that the person who self-harms receives at church will go a long way to building their confidence in recovery and their belief in life and their faith in God. When asked about church one self-harmer said: 'It needs to be a place where I can feel secure and safe despite what is going on in my life.' How would you describe your church? Is there anything you can do to make it more accessible to emotionally wounded people like self-harmers? The following are worth considering:

Make church welcoming. Ensure that people on the doors are sensitive to vulnerable people. There may need to be extra attention given to drawing people in who find relating more difficult.

Have leaflets and posters around which reflect the emotional needs of people as well as the spiritual, helping the self-harmer and others to feel that they are accepted.

Ensure that child protection and vulnerable adults policies are displayed in a public place in church, with someone to oversee them and ensure that they are kept up-to-date, and be a contact for people with concerns.

Be clear about your procedure when someone does disclose that they self-harm (or have any other emotional or mental health needs). Are you in a position to offer help within the church or do you need to refer the person?

Be a loving community, willing to stick with a person through thick and thin, supporting them through their recovery journey even if not directly involved in the therapeutic care.

Set clear boundaries and be consistent. Let the person know what you can and can't do to help and don't endeavour to do something that then has to be retracted as it will fuel feelings of rejection and being let down.

A MESSAGE FOR ALL

The additional tips below are not only for leaders; they are for anyone in the church. If these are followed through they will make a big difference. The person who self-harms will feel safer and no doubt be more responsive when approached.

Helpful tips
- See the person as an individual, not as a self-harmer.
- Build up a relationship of trust before asking too many questions.
- Let the person express their fears and doubts about God.
- Don't over-spiritualise or instantly try to solve the person's problems.
- Don't assume that the issue is demonic or that the person isn't a Christian.
- If prayer is offered, it needs to be with people who have insight into self-harm.
- Include the person – don't allow self-harm to become a reason to leave them out.
- Be mindful that the word 'blood' can act as a trigger (even phrases such as 'the Blood of Jesus'; 'blood sacrifice'; 'His blood paid the price for our sin').
- Inform people when using graphic images in presentations – some portrayals of the crucifixion can be triggering, as can certain noises.
- If offering prayer at the end of, or during, a service or meeting,

be careful not to open up painful issues and leave the person in a vulnerable state.

- Be clear about what follow up can be offered as a result of a person being affected (positively or negatively) in church.
- Keep confidences – don't talk to others so they can pray without the self-harmer knowing.
- Be well informed: the leaflet 'Promoting a Safe Church' is very helpful.[1]

AVAILABLE HELP

There are different types of help that can be offered within a church setting and it is important to be clear about which of these are available and what is involved. These include befriending, Christian counselling and prayer ministry. Sometimes people use the words in very loose terms, 'I'm counselling the girl who joined us a few weeks ago', when what they are actually doing is 'befriending'. Counselling and prayer ministry are types of help for which there should be training and supervision. The person being helped may not know the difference and receive counselling at church that is out of context and carried out by someone unqualified to help in this way. Sadly, it is in these situations that people have often been hurt or wounded because the helper is extending themselves beyond their limits.

Befriending

Jerusha Clark, author of *Inside a Cutter's Mind,*[2] says, 'Through His life, Christ taught that being with people who are hurting *matters.* We all know that it's easier to ignore the hurt in other people than it is to get into the pit with them. But Christ models how to, and challenges us to give and receive the ministry of presence.' By just *being* with people, regardless of anything we do or say, we communicate to them that they are worthy of our time. Here are some befriending tips:

Be a good listener. In Chapter 2 we said that self-harm has its own voice – try to hear that voice in the person who is sharing with you. Make yourself available to them when you can, whilst keeping appropriate boundaries.

Be a role model. Allow yourself to deal with your own feelings instead of bottling them up inside. Setting boundaries around how you support them, eg how late at night they can call or how much of the weekend they can spend with you, shows them the importance of valuing yourself, family and time.

Be a friend. Don't leave them out of your social life, or only have interest in them as a sufferer. Build up trust in one another – relationships are two-way. Valuing someone enough to share your life with them as well as listening to their issues is a great self-esteem builder.

Be patient. Don't force your opinions and goals on them. The more you push them to stop, the more they will feel overly pressured and will be less likely to trust you.

Be practical. Consider ways in which you can practically support the person without taking away their autonomy. You may be able to help look up information on support groups, therapists and talks. If the person finds a particular task, such as filling in forms, difficult, you could lend a hand.

Offer the love of Christ. 1 Corinthians 13:13 says 'But the greatest of these is love.' Above all else you can show love to someone. This means accepting, not judging; valuing, and not having unrealistic expectations.

Christian counselling

When offering counselling in the church it is helpful to explain upfront the approach carried out. Put very simply, Christian counselling falls into one of two categories. One is secular counselling, carried out by a Christian. The other is counselling based on a biblical model that addresses the spiritual and emotional aspects of the problem. The client's relationship with God plays an integral role.

If you are a counsellor seeing someone who self-harms, the information in Chapter 11 will be particularly relevant.

Prayer Ministry

It's important to distinguish between prayer ministry time (ministry that takes part during/after church services) and prayer ministry appointments (in-depth ministry carried out by trained prayer ministers during a pre-arranged time, usually over a number of sessions). Prayer ministry has the emphasis of listening to God and allowing Him to identify the areas of a person's life that need healing, as well as dealing with spiritual problems.

THE SPIRITUAL ELEMENT

Whilst we have seen throughout the book that self-harm is largely a coping mechanism put into place as a result of emotional woundedness, there is also a spiritual element. One of the key stumbling blocks is often forgiveness.

Forgiveness is a crucial part of recovery but unless the person raises it, be careful not to talk through the concept until you have built a relationship of trust, giving the person plenty of time to express their fears and concerns. Besides forgiving others, it is vital to look at the need for the person to forgive themselves. Their trauma history and shame as well as their guilt over some of the things they have done to themselves will inevitably lead them into a place of self-rejection and beliefs about being unforgiveable.

Approach to forgiveness

When we have been so hurt, especially by someone who was supposed to love and nurture us, the idea of forgiving them is incomprehensible to our human minds. And yet, that is what God requires us to do. The Bible says in Matthew 6:14–15: 'For if you forgive men when they sin against you, your heavenly Father will also forgive you. But if you do not forgive men their sins, your Father will not forgive your sins.' Sounds impossible, doesn't it? But let's look at some truths about forgiveness.

God understands how we feel. He doesn't gloss over the fact that we've been hurt. In fact, He knows and also understands what it feels like – Jesus was betrayed, tempted, abused, deserted, beaten, ridiculed, and killed. He understands our pain and that's why He wants us to be free of it.

Not forgiving others affects our relationship with God. Not forgiving someone won't affect our salvation (God's free gift to us when we surrender to Jesus and choose to follow Him) but it will affect our relationship with God now and allow the enemy to attack. If we are concentrating more on those who have hurt us than on the One who has saved us, we are missing out on so much.

Forgiving others is not first and foremost for their benefit. When someone hurts us we are linked to that person through the wound. By not forgiving, we stay linked to them and their wrongdoing. Many people believe that by forgiving the person they are letting them off the hook; quite the opposite, you are *freeing yourself*. It is not your job to bring justice; it's God's. Let Him deal with the person's wrongdoings.

Until we forgive, we can't see how God has shaped us through the hurts. If we love the Lord and want to be more like Jesus then the painful moments in life play a significant part. The Bible likens us to pure metals (gold and silver); their beauty is forged through a refining process (fire and hammers) and it's the same for us. If we haven't forgiven, we lose the opportunity to be shaped by the Lord. Forgiveness gives us the freedom to be able to say, 'This happened to me, but it doesn't define me, and it doesn't cause me pain any more.' When it comes to forgiving those who have hurt us, the only people necessary to make the transaction are you and God. However, bringing hurts to mind can be a painful process, so it might help to pray with the person, suggesting they use the following prayer:

Heavenly Father, You know the painful events that I have been through. It both hurts and has affected my life. I ask that you heal me. I choose to forgive _____ for _____ and all their acts of unkindness. I leave them in Your hands. Renew my mind to think positively about life and about myself and deliver me from oppression by the enemy. I ask this in Jesus' Name. Amen.

Forgiving ourselves

The flipside of forgiving those who have sinned against us is forgiving ourselves and accepting forgiveness from the only One who can truly forgive. If God, who created the universe, says He forgives us then who are we not to do the same! Forgiveness is the only way to experience the fullness of God's plan for our lives.

REFLECTION

Churches should be at the forefront of dealing with the mentally ill and emotionally distressed. Jesus was a trailblazer, not someone following behind.

ACTION

What can you do to make your church a place where people feel safe and loved, despite what they are going through?

PRAYER

Dear God, Your Word says that anyone who comes to You can be free indeed, and live life to the full (John 10:10). Jesus, please would you help us treat people who come into our churches as You would treat them, showing them that they are welcome, accepted and loved. Amen

FINAL WORDS

We have come to the end of our time together looking at self-harm. We (Helena and Abbie) hope that *Insight into Self-Harm* has given you just that, *insight*, and that you feel better equipped to help self-harmers (if you are family or carer) and motivated to keep seeking recovery (if you are a self-harmer). Don't give up hope!

For information on Helena's writing and speaking visit:
www.helenawilkinson.co.uk

RESOURCES

BOOKS

Secret Scars, Abigail Robson, Authentic Media – the author's story.

Inside a Cutter's Mind by Jerusha Clark and Dr Earl Henslin, NavPress – a comprehensive consideration of self-harming from a Christian perspective.

Crying Scarlet Tears, Sophie Scott, Monarch Books – an autobiography with chapters on understanding the issue and trying to help others.

WEBSITES

Adullam Ministries: www.adullam-ministries.org.uk
An online information site, with a forum for support.

Think Twice – www.thinktwiceinfo.org
Aims to increase awareness of mental health issues through providing expert speakers and writers for events and media publications.

Self Harm UK – www.selfharm.co.uk A safe, pro-recovery site for young people plus a multimedia training programme.

HELPLINES

Samaritans: 08457 90 90 90 (UK) 1850 60 90 90 (ROI).
www.samaritans.org

ChildLine: 0800 1111. A 24-hour listening service for those under 16.

Crossline: 0300 111 0101 a confidential, Christian-staffed helpline
www.crossline.org.uk

COUNSELLING

CWR offers a counselling refferal service. Contact Jenifer Jones on 01344 893197.

The Association of Christian Counsellors has a list of counsellors and counselling organisations across the country. Go to www.acc-uk.org for details.

NOTES

CHAPTER 1

1. www.mentalhealth.org.uk/help-information/mental-health-a-z/S/self-harm
2. *Diagnostic and Statistical Manual of Mental Disorders* (American Psychiatric Publishing, 2013)
3. Matthew K. Nock 'Self-Injury', *Annual Review of Clinical Psychology*, Vol. 6 April 2010, pp339–363.

CHAPTER 2

1. www.self-injury.net/media/famous-self-injurers
2. www.rcpsych.ac.uk/expertadvice/problemsdisorders/self-harm.aspx
3. Jan Sutton, *Healing the Hurt Within*, (Oxford: How To Books Ltd, 2007)
4. www.mind.org.uk/mental_health_a-z/7985_how_to_deal_with_anger

CHAPTER 3

1. Adapted from onlinecounsellingcollege.com (The 7 Emotional Needs of Children)
2. Helena Wilkinson, *Insight into Eating Disorders* (Farnham: CWR, 2006)
2. Helena Wilkinson, *Beyond Chaotic Eating* (Weybridge: RoperPenberthy Publishing Ltd, 2009)
3. Adapted from National Institute for Health and Clinical Excellence [NICE] 2009
4. Helena Wilkinson, *Insight into Child and Adult Bullying* (Farnham: CWR, 2013) pp85–86)

CHAPTER 4

1. Jerusha Clark and Dr Earl Henslin, *Inside a Cutter's Mind* (Colorado Springs: NavPress Publishing Group, 2007)

CHAPTER 5

1. www.helpguide.org/mental/self_injury.htm
2. www.bacp.co.uk

CHAPTER 6

1. Doran, G.T. (1981), There's a S.M.A.R.T. way to write management's goals and objectives, Management Review, Volume 70, Issue II (AMA FORUM) pp 35-36.
2. www.helpguide.org/mental/self_injury.htm

CHAPTER 8

1. Dr A. Ellis, *Reason and Emotion in Psychotherapy* (Secaucus, New Jersey: Citadel Press, 1964)

CHAPTER 9

1. T. Knoster, R. Villa, and J. Thousand, (2000). A framework for thinking about systems change. In: R. Villa and J. Thousand (eds.) *Restructuring for Caring and Effective Education: Piecing the Puzzle Together* (Baltimore: Paul H. Brookes Publishing Co.) pp. 93-128
2. Helena Wilkinson, *Insight into Child and Adult Bullying* (Farnham: CWR, 2013) pp103-104, 107-112, 121-122
3. Helena Wilkinson, *Breaking Free from Loneliness* (Weybridge: RoperPenberthy Publishing Ltd, 2004)

CHAPTER 10

1. Jerusha Clark and Dr Earl Henslin, *Inside a Cutter's Mind* (Colorado Springs: NavPress Publishing Group, 2007)
2. www.nspcc.org.uk/help-and-advice/for-parents-and-carers/parenting-advice/self-harming_wda94588.html

CHAPTER 12

1. www.churchofengland.org/media/37405/promotingasafechurch.pdf
2. Jerusha Clark and Dr Earl Henslin, *Inside a Cutter's Mind* (Colorado Springs: NavPress Publishing Group, 2007)

Courses and seminars

Publishing and media

Conference facilities

Transforming lives

CWR's vision is to enable people to experience personal transformation through applying God's Word to their lives and relationships.

Our Bible-based training and resources help people around the world to:
• Grow in their walk with God
• Understand and apply Scripture to their lives
• Resource themselves and their church
• Develop pastoral care and counselling skills
• Train for leadership
• Strengthen relationships, marriage and family life
and much more.

Our insightful writers provide daily Bible-reading notes and other resources for all ages, and our experienced course designers and presenters have gained an international reputation for excellence and effectiveness.

CWR's Training and Conference Centres in Surrey and East Sussex, England, provide excellent facilities in idyllic settings – ideal for both learning and spiritual refreshment.

CWR Applying God's Word
to everyday life and relationships

CWR, Waverley Abbey House,
Waverley Lane, Farnham,
Surrey GU9 8EP, UK

Telephone: **+44 (0)1252 784700**
Email: info@cwr.org.uk
Website: www.cwr.org.uk

Registered Charity No 294387
Company Registration No 1990308

Insight series

Handling issues that are feared, ignored or misunderstood.

Explore our full range of Insight books and courses

BOOKS

Insight into Self-Esteem
by Chris Ledger and Wendy Bray
ISBN: 978-1-85345-663-3

Insight into Child and Adult Bullying
by Helena Wilkinson
ISBN: 978-1-85345-912-2

Insight into Helping Survivors of Childhood Sexual Abuse
by Wendy Bray and Heather Churchill
ISBN: 978-1-85345-692-3

Insight into Addiction
by Andre Radmall
ISBN: 978-1-85345-661-9

 ALSO AVAILABLE AS EBOOK/KINDLE

For a complete list of the 15 titles available in this series visit
www.cwr.org.uk/insight
Available online or from a Christian bookshop.

COURSES

These invaluable teaching days are designed both for those who would like to come for their own benefit and for others who seek to support people facing particular issues.

For the latest course information and dates about CWR's one-day Insight seminars visit
www.cwr.org.uk/insightdays

STAY IN TOUCH
@CWRInsight
#cwrinsight
www.cwr.org.uk/insight